THE PRIEST OF THE FATHERS

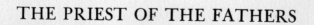

The Priest
of the Fathers

by

Edward L. Heston, C.S.C.

THE BRUCE PUBLISHING COMPANY
MILWAUKEE

Nihil obstat: REV. KERNDT M. HEALY, C.S.C.
Imprimi potest: REV. THOMAS A. STEINER, C.S.C., Provincial
Nihil obstat: H. B. RIES, Censor librorum
Imprimatur: ✠ MOSES E. KILEY, Archbishop of Milwaukee

May 5, 1945

Preface

A HEARTY welcome always greets any book on the priesthood which brings or recalls to us rich and fruitful thoughts. Such is the volume *The Priest of the Fathers,* which the Reverend Edward L. Heston, C.S.C., offers to the public, and to priests in particular, as the fruit of his studies and meditations on the Fathers and Doctors of the Church.

These great champions of our Faith treat of the priesthood with a profound sense of spirituality. The priest is clothed with such exalted dignity and endowed with powers of such magnitude that he has a special claim to be called *divinitatis particeps.* The Angelic Doctor, St. Thomas Aquinas, observes that if we consider creatures in themselves, a higher degree of perfection in them is always conceivable. But if we regard them in the light of their relationship to God, the Uncreated Good, they may acquire a certain infinity from the Infinite Being. The great Doctor then illustrates his thought by pointing out that such is the case with the Blessed Virgin, according as she is the Mother of God; with grace, inasmuch as it brings us near to God, and with the universe, according as it exists for the glory of God (*I Sent.* dist. 44, q. 1, art. 3). The same can be said of the greatness and dignity of the Catholic priesthood.

By means of sanctifying grace men become *divinitatis participes.* In the priesthood, the manner of this divine elevation is both marvelous and truly sublime. Proof and pledge of this nobility are found in the Holy Sacrifice of the Mass which the priest continually offers, in the administration of the Sacraments, and in the sacred ministry which is entrusted to him. His is not the greatness of men, nor the glory of earth.

The dignity or grandeur of the priest must of necessity rest on the indispensable foundation of deep, sincere humility, and avail itself of all the precautions and means to safeguard this virtue. The priest must practise humility of mind, of heart, and even of body. The first manifestation and first step in the practice of this virtue is discerned in obedience. On the foundation of these virtues of humility and obedience the priest builds and expands his activity and mission. Without them, whatever may be the richness of his natural talent, he will be unable to protect his real greatness, and will even end by losing it.

Here we find our guiding light in the very earliest example of priestly formation known to us. The Divine Founder of the Church opened and conducted the first Seminary; He wished to have His Apostles continually at His side. It was His intention that they should hear the Gospel from His own lips, behold His own example, and study the means of imitating Him, in order that they in turn might form their own followers along

these same divine lines. The pages of the New Testament have brought down to us the essence of this
divine and apostolic teaching, and the clergy of every
age and every country has molded its ideals on this
doctrine and these traditions.

* * *

The Fathers of the Church were the principal chan-
nels through which the priestly message of the New
Testament was faithfully handed down to us and il-
lustrated with practical applications. After them came
the Doctors of the Church. In their treatment of the
most important points of Christian dogma and moral,
these trustworthy witnesses of our early traditions could
not neglect the priesthood; to this theme they dedi-
cated golden pages which admirably echo the voices
of apostolic times. Their very names spell greatness:
Ignatius of Antioch, Cyprian, John Chrysostom, Ambrose, Jerome, Augustine, Gregory the Great, Leo the
Great, and, in later years, Bernard and others.

In his present volume Dr. Heston has not compiled
a mere anthology of patristic texts on the priesthood.
Rather he has selected and woven together a beautiful
series of passages dealing with priestly life and work,
and to them has added timely comments. His book
thus portrays the greatness of the priesthood, as seen
through the eyes of the Fathers, and applied to the
priest's duties to God, his neighbor, and himself.

* * *

First of all, the Fathers picture the priest as the

representative left by Christ on His return to heaven, to take His place in looking after the interests of His Heavenly Father and carrying on His work. In union with Christ Himself, and through the powers received at ordination, the priest looses and binds sins, and perpetuates the Eucharistic Sacrifice. He is the chosen spokesman of our Lord and, so to speak, must be a living embodiment of His Gospel. Only in this way will he continue the work of building the Church, which is "the pillar and mainstay of the truth" (I Tim. 3:15).

The Fathers explain that by the very fact of perpetuating the immolation of the Son of God, the priest must, like Christ, sacrifice himself for the salvation of souls. From God come the priest's dignity and powers, and to God in return he must give his most cherished possession, namely, himself. In addition, we can see how the mind of the Fathers is clear as to the manner in which the priest must live — his must be a life of generous and total consecration to works of piety and charity. He is the father of souls, not their master; a spiritual leader, and yet a servant; foreign to the business and interests of men, and still devoted to the individual welfare of each one of his faithful and thus of society at large, for the priesthood is likewise a social office. The priest of God must be meek, humble, charitable, and withal strong in the defense of justice. It is his duty to take the lead in giving good example, in order to secure for souls the first places in the Kingdom of God. For all these reasons Christ has bestowed on His priest a primacy of dignity.

Furthermore, declare these great lights of the Church, it is only in nearness to the Throne of God that the minister of Christ can live a good priestly life. This life must be preceded by solid formation. Only after serious training can the candidate for Orders offer to the priesthood all his natural gifts, as the foundation whereon the supernatural will build and develop. These years of formation are to be marked by constant and fervent discipline of mind and heart through study and training in virtue, by a fearless spirit of sacrifice, and diligence in acquiring experience of things both human and divine. Ordination takes the priest to the altar, and as he there offers with Christ the Divine Sacrifice he becomes a confidant of the Divine Master: "No longer do I call you servants. . . . But I have called you friends, because all things that I have heard from my Father, I have made known to you" (John 15:15). In this closeness to the Throne of God he steels himself for the accomplishment of his exalted duties.

The sublime thoughts of the Fathers leave us with a vibrant and lasting impression. Their words are evidently the genuine echo of that teaching of which our Divine Master said: "My teaching is not my own, but his that sent Me" (John 7:16). For this reason, may this book meet with a warm welcome. May the reading of it be a new fountainhead of that priestly fervor which the Sovereign Pontiff, Pope Pius XI, emphasized in his great Encyclical *Ad Catholici Sacerdotii* (December 20, 1935), and which the reigning Pontiff, Pope Pius XII, has never ceased to keep alive through his

noble pronouncements and his manifold provisions for
the sanctification of the clergy.

✠ AMLETO GIOVANNI CICOGNANI
Archbishop of Laodicea in Phrygia
Apostolic Delegate

Washington, D. C.
June 8, 1944
Feast of Corpus Christi

Author's Preface

THE priest occupies a central position in the Church. Because he is a mediator between God and man, his entire life points to these two terms of his priestly mission. As for every other creature, his primary duty is to his Maker. The center of his life is in "the things pertaining to God, that he may offer gifts and sacrifices for sins."[1] Nevertheless, because he is taken from among men and for men,[2] he is under obligation to those whose spiritual welfare is one of the chief reasons for his ordination. Lastly, but none the less fundamentally, he is under obligation to himself. "Because he himself also is beset with weakness,"[3] he owes it to himself and to his sacerdotal calling to become always less unworthy to stand before God as a suppliant for men.

This threefold aspect of priestly life and work suggests itself naturally as the general outline for the present study on the priest in the Fathers. Perhaps the twentieth-century mind will look askance and object that it is out of date to resurrect the Fathers from their peaceful resting-places on dusty library shelves. Particularly on such vital reality as the priesthood it may seem quite out of place to go back some fourteen or fifteen centuries to ferret out the ideals of Augustine, Greg-

ory, Leo, or Chrysostom for the ministers of God. From
the American priest of today, with his complex parish
work and varied activities, his associations with labor
difficulties and social problems, some may think it is
too far a cry back to the early ages of the faith when
priests and bishops seemingly had little else to do but
deliver exquisite homilies on feast days.

Nevertheless, no matter how varied may be the
duties of today's priest in an unstable world, the priesthood itself is eternal. The scenes of its activity will
necessarily shift with times and places, but its deep
reality is as changeless as the unending priesthood of
the eternal Son of God. Yet experience teaches that
even though a great reality remains always substan-
tially the same it is none the less in constant danger of
being obscured by inescapable stress on its changing
outward manifestations. For this reason it will be
profitable to inquire how our Fathers in the Church
portrayed the ideal minister of God. Their lessons,
based on the inner reality of the priesthood, have a
practical present-day application which they were perhaps far from suspecting and which we in turn may
never have realized. The zealous bishops and priests
of the early centuries are not so old-fashioned as one
might be led to suspect.

*   *   *

PART I, THE PRIEST AND GOD, aims to sketch the unchanging priestly ideal, the priest's relationship to
Christ, and the ideals which should inspire him as he
acquits himself of his duties to God at the altar of

sacrifice. In Part II, THE PRIEST AND THE PEOPLE,
stress is laid on the priest's responsibility for others,
the expression of this responsibility in a life of zeal,
the duty of good example, and the proper use of
priestly authority. Lastly, Part III, THE PRIEST AND
HIMSELF, turns the priest's attention to his general
duty of equipping himself for his apostolate by acquiring and developing a taste for sacred learning, safe-
guarding himself against the dangers of the world,
particularly those of avarice and sensuality, by developing a far-reaching spirit of sacrifice, and giving
serious reflection to his essential duty of saving his own
soul. Although preaching is one of the most fundamental priestly duties, no express treatment of it will
be found here. It is hoped that the abundant material
in the Fathers on this subject will constitute the content of a further study.

With but rare exceptions, which are indicated in
their respective places, only those texts have been used
which in the original were directly addressed to priests
or bishops. To compile a patristic commentary of texts
merely applicable to the priesthood would go far beyond the possibilities of even many volumes. No attempt has been made to collect all the patristic texts
referring to the priesthood, nor even to compile the
most striking. Because it is basically dependent on the
limitations imposed by the quantity of individual read-
ings and on selections determined by personal taste,
a study of this kind cannot pretend to be all-inclusive.

Unless otherwise indicated, all texts are taken from
the *Patrologia Latina* or the *Patrologia Graeca* of

Migne. For citations from St. John Chrysostom, however, reference is always to the Vivès edition (Paris, 1878) of the Greek-French text by Abbé Bareille.

Kind friends and helpful advisers have given generously of their time and talents in clearing the manuscript of many defects and inaccuracies. For their assistance they have a special claim on the gratitude of the reader. Their efficient cooperation has, in large measure, made it possible to present the message of the Fathers in the following pages.

Contents

PART I

THE PRIEST AND GOD

Chapter I

The Unchanging Priestly Ideal

THE general lineaments of the Catholic priesthood
were first traced out by St. Paul in the Epistle to
the Hebrews. The Apostle's descriptions of the eternal
High Priest of the New Law, and the ensuing con-
trasts with the inferior ministers of the Old Dispensation, betoken the ideal demanded of men who share
in the priesthood of their great Pontiff, the Man-God.
Verse 26 of Chapter VII, in which St. Paul speaks directly of our Lord, epitomizes the qualities to be
sought for in the priest of the New Law: "For it was
fitting that we should have such a high priest, holy,
innocent, undefiled, separated from sinners, and made
higher than the heavens."[1]

It would be expecting too much to search for a
perfect and unvarying echo of these inspired words
in all our early ecclesiastical writers. Nor would this
be to our purpose. The Pauline ideal of the priesthood lays particular stress on the personal qualities of
the priests of Christ; it says nothing explicit of the

influence exerted by these qualities in the actual work of the sacerdotal ministry. Still in the very first decades after the apostolic age, the first applications of St. Paul's ideal to the exigencies of the growing Church were well under way. With heresy and schism threatening from every side, the primary duty of the Church's official guardians was watchfulness; the first manifestation of the priestly ideal was in zealous vigilance for the unity and purity of faith. This is the burden of one of the first priestly exhortations on record. In the letter of Ignatius, Bishop of Antioch, to Polycarp, Bishop of Smyrna, in the closing years of the first century, we read: "I beseech you by the grace wherewith you are endowed, to increase your field of work and to exhort all men into salvation. Defend your position with every temporal and spiritual means available. Have an eye to unity, for nothing is better or more profitable. Always give others first place, as the Lord gives to you. Bear with all in charity, as you do. Devote yourself to unceasing prayer. Ask for greater wisdom than you now have. Keep watch in the possession of a sleepless spirit. Speak to each one according to God's custom. Bear with the ills of all as a perfect athlete. The greater your labor, the greater also will be your reward."[2]

This exhortation to sleepless vigilance and devotion to others shows how the ideal of the priest as mediator between heaven and earth had taken firm hold in the mind of the Church from the very beginning. As the representative of the one Mediator, Christ Jesus, the priest is answerable to God for the spiritual well-being

of all men. That is why St. Ignatius pleads with St.
Polycarp to "exhort all men unto salvation." On the
shoulders of every priest rests a collective responsibility
whereby he ceases to be a private individual and becomes instead a public personage. He is a minister of
eternal salvation for all men. St. John Chrysostom
bases all his requirements of holiness in the priest on
this special character as mediator: "How perfect
should be the man who pleads for the whole city? Did
I say 'for the whole city'? Rather, the priest pleads for
the entire world, and beseeches God to have mercy not
only on the sins of the living, but likewise on those of
the departed. I would say that not even all the confidence of Moses and Elias would be enough for this
intercession. For the priest goes before God as if the
whole world were entrusted to his keeping, and as
though he were the father of all men, praying that all
wars may be ended and all uprisings appeased, begging
for peace and prosperity and the elimination of all
public and private misfortunes. In all things he must
be so far superior to all those for whom he prays that
he will be a shining example to all who are under
him."[3]

In order to be worthy of this dignity as mediator
before God for his fellow men, the priest finds himself faced with the necessity of combating any evil
tendencies which can make him displeasing to God.
At the same time his ministry requires him to be con-
genial with his fellow men. Between these two sacred
duties he must strike the happy medium. He is under
obligation to eradicate his defects, in order to find

favor in the eyes of his Lord; at the same time he must take care to avoid any semblance of false and exaggerated virtue, lest he be suspected of insincerity. It is for this reason that the well-balanced priestly life seems almost to entail contradiction. These apparently contradictory obligations, however, tend only to emphasize in bolder relief the fundamental priestly office whereby a man becomes a point of contact between God and the world. Hence St. John Chrysostom sketches for us the following rapid outline of necessary priestly qualities:

"Consider for a moment the qualities to be sought in him who is charged with battling against the storms of the world and checking the different elements which are leagued against Christian society. He must be at the same time both serious-minded and unaffected; exacting and yet gentle; unyielding in his commands but considerate of everyone; impartial and ready to render service; humble yet in all things dignified; energetic and yet meek in order that he may triumph over all these opposing elements.

"With unyielding firmness of principle and notwithstanding all pressure, he must know how to promote worthy men to positions of dignity and how to reject all others, no matter how stubborn or how well organized may be the forces marshalled against him. Having in view only the edification of the Church, he should never wander away from this goal, whether out of love or out of hatred."[4]

Another glimpse of this same ideal is afforded by St. Gregory the Great in Book One of his *Regulae*

Pastoralis Liber: "Wherefore that man above all, should in every possible way be set up as a living example, who has died to all the passions of the flesh and now lives in the world of the spiritual; who has given up worldly prosperity, who fears no adversity, and has his desires set only on interior things, while neither bodily weakness nor mental rebellion counteracts these desires. Far from coveting the goods of others, he gives away his own. Through a merciful heart he is quickly inclined to forgive offences, but while not granting pardon more generously than is proper, he never surrenders the fortress of righteousness. Without ever doing unlawful things himself, he laments as his own the misdeeds of others. Out of the affection of his heart he has compassion on the weakness of others, and in this way he rejoices in their progress as in his own. In all his actions he makes himself such an example for others that at least he never has to blush for the past. He tries so to live that he may water with the streams of doctrine the parched hearts of his brethren.

"By his assiduous practice of prayer he has learned how to obtain his requests from the Lord, and through the pleasing affection of his voice he already hears the answer: 'Whilst thou art still crying, I shall say: Here I am!' If someone were to come to us and ask us to intercede for him with some powerful personage who is angry with him and yet unknown to us, we would answer immediately: 'I cannot plead for you before this man, because I do not know him well enough.' If men, therefore, are ashamed in ordinary life to intercede for others before those whom they do not know, how can anyone be so bold as to lay hold of a position of intercession for the people before God without being sure that he is close to His grace through the merit of a good life? Or how can anyone ask pardon for others, if he is not sure himself of being in good standing?

"And in this connection there are still greater grounds for fear lest he who is thought fit to placate the anger of God should rather merit punishment through his own guilt. All reason very well that when a *persona non grata* is sent as mediator, those who are already angry become angered still more. Let him, therefore, who is still entangled in earthly desires beware lest he heap still more abundant fuel on the wrath of our severe Judge and lest, by glorying in his exalted position, he bring down ruin upon his subjects."[5]

The high regard entertained in ecclesiastical circles for this classic of St. Gregory the Great on priestly life and practice is evidenced by the following advice of Blessed Alcuin to Simeon, a missionary priest in England: "Wherever you go, the book of St. Gregory on the pastoral life should accompany you. Read it and re-read it frequently in order that in it you may come to know yourself and the work you have to do, and keep before your mind how you should live and teach. For this book is a mirror of priestly life and a medicine for all the wounds of the devil's deceits."[6]

Six centuries after this passage was penned by St. Gregory we find the same ideal portrayed in still

greater detail by St. Bernard of Clairvaux. It is true
that in the following passage the Abbot of Clairvaux
addresses himself directly to Pope Eugenius, and that
the specific points which he enumerates are applicable
in their entirety only to the Sovereign Pontiff. Yet
much of what he says applies to priests in general,
since the office of Supreme Pastor crystallizes in an
eminent degree all the qualities and distinctions with
which even the humble priest should always be endowed. St. Bernard depicts as follows the priestly
mentality for Pope Eugenius: "The mind that is devoted to such great and so many interests should be
devoid of anxiety over lowly and minor interests. It
should be *free,* with no violent occupation claiming
its attention. It should be *noble,* not degraded by any
unworthy affection, and *righteous,* so as not to be influenced by any questionable motive. It should be
cautious, lest it fall victim to furtive suspicion; *watchful,* so as not to be distracted by wandering and curious
thoughts, and *steadfast,* lest it be shaken by sudden
excitement. Finally, it should be *invincible,* so as not
to be weakened by continual tribulation; and *spacious,*
lest it be shrunken by the loss of temporal goods."[7]

Later on the saint becomes much more specific in
delineating the qualities of the perfect sacerdotal ideal:
"Bear in mind that the Holy Roman Church of which
you, under the guidance of God, are the ruler, is the
Mother of all the churches, not their mistress; that
you are not lord of bishops, but one of their number;
that you are the brother of those who love God and
the companion of all who fear Him. Remember that

you must be a model of justice, a mirror of holiness and an example of piety, champion of the truth, defender of the faith, teacher of the nations, the leader of Christians, a friend of the Bridegroom, an attendant of the Bride, the director of the clergy, the shepherd of the people, the teacher of the ignorant, the refuge of the oppressed, the advocate of the poor, the hope of the wretched, the guardian of orphans, the judge of widows, the eye of the blind, the tongue of the dumb, the staff of the old, the avenger of crimes, the terror of the wicked, the glory of the righteous, the sceptre of the mighty, the hammer of tyrants, the father of kings, the moderator of laws, the light of the world, a priest of the Most High, the vicar of Christ, the anointed of the Lord.

"Understand what I tell you, for the Lord will give you wisdom. Where a proneness to evil is linked with a position of power, you must rely for strength on something above men. Let your face be turned upon evildoers. Let him who has no regard for men and no fear of the sword, at least stand in awe at the breath of thy anger. If he rejects all warnings, let him fear the power of your prayer, and realize that your anger against anyone really unleashes the wrath of God and not merely of man. Whosoever will not hearken to you, should dread the prospect of having to hearken to God speaking against him."[8]

Two centuries later, in a passage which is strongly reminiscent of St. Gregory the Great, St. Thomas Aquinas expresses very concisely the priest's need of careful attention to the things of God at the same time that he endeavors to make himself "all things to all men:"

"There are two duties of pastors, namely, that they should be lofty in their knowledge of divine things, and zealous in the activities connected with things religious. For their subjects must be instructed in the faith, and this calls for wisdom. Hence the Apostle says: 'in all wisdom' (And I shall give you words and understanding against which all your adversaries will be unable to contradict). Likewise these same subjects must be directed in their external actions. This calls for prudence to direct outside activity, and for this reason the Apostle mentions prudence. (Be ye therefore prudent.)

"Thus we see what advantages the Apostles enjoy with regard to the excellence of their wisdom. Then there follows their advantage with respect to revelation, where the Apostle says: '. . . that he might make known the sacrament, etc.' as though he said: 'Our wisdom is not of the secrets of nature, nor of the courses of stars and the like, but our knowledge is in Christ alone.' "[9]

The rapid sketch in the preceding pages aims to point out the unchanging character of the ideal of the Catholic priesthood. From Ignatius about to be devoured by wild beasts to Polycarp tortured at the stake, on to Gregory the Great snatched from his beloved monastic solitude to the government of the Universal Church, and from him to Bernard of Clairvaux composing in his wild hermitage an inspiring exhortation for the Head of the Church, the ideal remains the same: Christ is the one Mediator of God and man. The priest is Christ's other self — another Christ.

From St. Bernard we might page through the tomes of many other Doctors of the Church or ecclesiastical writers, such as St. Bonaventure, Cardinal de Bérulle, M. Olier, St. Vincent de Paul, or St. Alphonsus de Liguori. We would find the selfsame doctrine passed on from one generation of holy priests to another. But to conclude this portrayal of the priestly ideal we may cite the authoritative words of our late Holy Father, Pope Pius XI, in his celebrated encyclical *Ad Catholici Sacerdotii:*

"A priest should have a loftiness of spirit, a purity of heart and a sanctity of life befitting the solemnity and the holiness of the office which he holds. For this, as we have said, makes the priest a mediator between God and man, a mediator in the place and by the command of Him who is the 'one mediator of God and man, the man, Jesus Christ.' The priest must, therefore, approach as closely as possible to the perfection of Him whose vicar he is, and render himself ever more and more pleasing to God, by the sanctity of his life and deeds. More than the scent of incense or the beauty of churches and altars, God loves and accepts holiness. 'They who are the intermediaries between God and His people,' says St. Thomas, 'must bear a good conscience before God and a good name among men.' On the contrary, whosoever handles and administers holy things while blameworthy in his life, profanes them and is guilty of sacrilege. 'They who are not holy ought not to handle holy things.'"

The substance of the ideal of the eternal priesthood, then, remains forever the same. The minister of God today in the large cities or the isolated mission posts of the United States must, no less than Polycarp at Smyrna, exhort all men unto salvation, keep watch in the possession of a sleepless spirit, bear with all men in charity, and devote himself to unceasing prayer. With the ideal priest of St. John Chrysostom he must realize that the whole world is entrusted to his keeping and so comport himself as if he were the father of all men. No less than the priest of Gregory the Great, his vocation is so to live that he may water with refreshing streams of doctrine the parched hearts of his brethren and by the assiduous practice of prayer obtain peace and prosperity and all other good things for those under him. Even more today than in the days of St. Bernard, the faithful priest is called upon to develop a mind and a will which are free, noble, righteous, cautious, watchful, steadfast, and invincible, so that his enemies and God's enemies may live in continual and salutary dread of his reproofs. In our age particularly the priest must heed St. Thomas' admonition to have a good conscience before God and a good name among men. Even for the seemingly different practical aspects of priestly life and activity of today, we can find in our Fathers many practical lessons, all the more valuable for being in such close contact with the unchanging ideal of Christ. The Fathers' ideal of the priesthood has not grown old or outmoded with the centuries, because it is the ideal of Christ, the eternal High Priest.

Chapter II

The Priest and Christ

IN HIS commentary on Chapter IV, verse 11, of the Epistle to the Ephesians, St. Thomas Aquinas points out that St. Paul gives the Apostles first place in his enumeration of Christ's gifts to the Church. The Apostles, he says, hold a privileged place among the gifts of Christ. They were characterized by a fullness of grace and wisdom and a wealth of eloquence, and were endowed with power and authority to govern the flock of Christ.[1] In a word, those charged with the care of souls are Christ's best gifts to the Church precisely because they are lasting, living continuations of Himself.

In recent years there has been rather extended discussion on the use of the term "other Christ" by the Fathers.[2] We know that this expression was applied by the Fathers, and often with striking realism, to the unordained Christian.[3] Whether or not the explicit term was likewise extended to the priest may perhaps be disputed. There can be no doubt, however, that the idea of *sacerdos, alter Christus* inspires the substance of all patristic writings on the dignity of the priesthood.

In commenting on the opening verses of the Epistle

to the Hebrews, St. John Chrysostom bases the superiority of the New Law over the Old on the superiority of the Man-God over the angels and prophets. The ministers of the Old Testament, he says, were in contact only with God's servants, "whereas we have hearkened to the voice of the Master Himself."[4] This closeness to Christ explains why St. Paul could sum up his entire apostolate by saying that the Son of God had been revealed in him.[5] On this passage St. John Chrysostom writes: "Instead of saying that the Son has been revealed to him, why does the Apostle say that the Son has been revealed *in* him? He says this to show that he has not received the teachings of faith merely by word of mouth. In these words he points out that he has been showered with spiritual gifts, that his soul has been enlightened with the splendor of revelation, that he has Christ Himself speaking within him."[6]

This master idea flows mainly from the consideration of the priest as the servant or minister of the Eternal Pontiff in heaven. The priesthood of the Son of God is eternal. Although He offered His oblation once, the everlasting efficacy of His unique sacrifice is made available to human souls through the ministration of His priests. Consequently these ministers are brought into close contact with the priestly offering of the Man-God. In the words of St. John Chrysostom: "Do not think, then, that because our Lord is a priest, He is always accomplishing the duties of His priesthood. He discharged this duty once, and then He returned to His throne in heaven. You must not imagine that in heaven He remains standing and is a minister of sacrifice. That is now the function of His servants."[7]

If the priest has functions which continue the work of Christ, it is but natural to suppose that he is endowed with whatever power and authority these functions demand. An all-wise God could not dispatch men on a divine mission without first equipping them with all the implements of their unique supernatural work. In order to impress upon them the realization of the heavenly ministry assigned to them, our Lord, as John Chrysostom remarks, sent the Apostles on their mission only after they had witnessed many striking miracles. This mission of the Apostles, the same saint continues, did not consist in an empty show of works, but was based on a genuinely divine transmission of power: "Our Lord was not content with merely encouraging His Apostles by calling their ministry a harvest. He went farther and strengthened them by giving them power to reap this harvest."[8]

This power is conferred at ordination. Though it is essentially spiritual, it is not restricted exclusively to the spiritual realm. Rather should we say that this power spiritualizes every aspect of priestly life. It is thus that St. John Chrysostom describes the efficacy of the liturgical prayers of the ordination ceremony: "By this means spiritual benefits are transmitted. In the strength of this prayer journeys are undertaken, and through this same prayer the priest receives the ministry of the Word."[9]

Again St. John shows how close the work of the

ministry brings the priest to Christ: "No one can say that after receiving the imposition of hands I have been wanting in my duty. Nevertheless this is not my doing, but the work of Christ."[10]

St. Leo declares even more explicitly: "Consequently, dearly beloved, it is not with bold presumption that, while mindful of divine goodness, we honor the day on which we accepted the office of High Priest. For we confess in all gratitude and truth that in whatever good we may do in the exercise of our ministry, it is Christ Himself who works in us."[11]

By the very nature of the sacerdotal mission and through the efficacy of the sacramental grace of Holy Orders, the priest carries on the work of Christ in the person of Christ. There is, of course, no confusion of personalities between him and his Lord. Each one contributes something of his own. As St. Augustine points out so concisely: "The disciples of the Lord offered Him the ministry of their bodies, while He in turn bestowed upon them the help of His divine majesty."[12]

Through the help of this divine majesty the priest acquires a oneness with the Man-God which sets him off in a class by himself. On the day of his ordination he is reminded that his priesthood gives him power over the real Body of Christ in the Holy Eucharist and over His Mystical Body in the Church. St. Jerome appeals to the consecration of the Body of Christ as to the chief source of priestly dignity. He then adds that through the priests of the Church we become

Christians.[13] In another passage he emphasizes the parallel between the priest and Christ when he writes that we are made sons of God through our Lord.

St. John Chrysostom goes even further, and makes the whole of the Christian life depend on the priesthood. There were, of course, no restrictions on the various methods which the Man-God might have chosen to insure the transmission of the divine life of grace to redeemed man. The fact of the matter is, however, that He chose a sacramental system of grace administered by priests, not only as the normal means of incorporation into His mystical body but as the source of all spiritual growth and progress. Hence no one becomes a Christian except through the ministry of the priests: "Do you not know that the priest is the angel of God. He never speaks merely in his own name. To disregard him means disregarding God Himself who appointed him His Minister. You will perhaps ask me how I prove that he has been appointed by God. If you do not believe this, then all your hope is in vain. If God does not work through the priest, then there is no forgiveness of sin, you have no part in the sacred mysteries, you receive no blessings — in a word, you are not a Christian."[14]

In another place he develops this same thought more in detail when he writes: "It is the work of the priest to beget new children unto God by Baptism. It is by the hand of the priest that we are clothed with Christ, that we are buried with Him and become members of His mystical body, of that body of which He is the Head. . . . To our priests we owe our birth unto divine life, for it is they who have given us true happiness, genuine liberty, and that heavenly adoption which has its root in grace."[15]

By making the sacramental actions of the priest the cause of "the heavenly adoption which has its root in grace," St. John Chrysostom eloquently professes his conviction of something more than a vague, moral unity between the priest and Christ. He ascribes to the priest the conferring of divine sonship which, St. John tells us in his Gospel[16] was the effect of the Incarnation. The perfection of this oneness is so profound and transforming that in his functions, particularly at the altar of sacrifice, the priest takes on the very person of the great High Priest whose minister he is: "When you behold the priest offering the consecrated bread, see in his hand the hand of Christ Himself."[17]

Then in Book Four of his treatise on the priesthood the same saint stresses the closeness of the priest to Christ even more graphically when he compares the sacrifice of the Old Law with the Holocaust of the Altar. After pointing out that the difference between the Mass and the Jewish offerings is gauged by the difference between Christ and the material oblations of the temple, he continues: "It is not wheat nor barley, oxen nor sheep, nor anything of the kind, but rather the very Body of Christ which is entrusted to you. In fact, according to the admirable teaching of St. Paul, the Church of Christ is the Body of Christ. Hence the guardian of this Body must work with unremitting zeal to clothe it with rich adornment and to preserve its heavenly beauty untarnished. He must be constantly on his guard lest spot, or wrinkle, or stain of any kind dull its splendor or lessen its perfection. His sole concern will be, as far as human weakness can realize this goal, to make this Body worthy of the sacred and immortal Head which gives it life."[18]

Thus St. John Chrysostom climaxes his insistence on the priest's closeness with our Lord by establishing a perfect parallel between the work of the priest and the mission of Christ to the Church as portrayed by St. Paul.[19] Our Lord turns over His own work of sanctification to His priests. This divine commission is contained in the sacramental grace of Holy Orders which makes possible the faithful accomplishment of such a charge. Thanks to this particular grace the priest acts in the name and in the person of Christ Himself, even to the extent that the normal spiritual life of the Church is left dependent on the ministrations of her priests. They carry on the life and work of Christ. Theirs is the life and work of the Man-God. They aim at the same goal and employ the same means to make the Church worthy of the immortal Head whence comes its life. There can be no more conclusive proof from the Fathers that the priest is another Christ.

Chapter III

The Priest at the Altar

S T. JOHN CHRYSOSTOM epitomizes the sacerdotal ideal when he describes the true priest as
one who will "minister according to the Spirit, and
model his life on the life of Christ."[1] The realization
of this sublime ideal is climaxed when the priest takes
his place at the altar. In the Sacrifice of the Mass he
rises to the peak of his relations with God. As he presents to the Father the Perfect Gift, he draws so close
to God as to speak and act in the name and in the person of the Son of God.

It is evident that such an exalted position and sacred
office demand a high degree of holiness. It is to be
expected also that familiarity with the spiritual realities of his sacerdotal functions will make the priest
even more holy by drawing him away from the spirit
of the world and closer to the spirit of God. It was this
realization which prompted St. John Chrysostom to
write that "the minister of God, whoever he may be,
finds in his sacred functions a power which draws him
away from evil and at the same time elevates him to a
plane of nobility."[2]

This special force for goodness and nobility which is found in priestly functions might possibly be compared with the sanctifying power of the Sacraments. The similarity would be verified particularly in the connection between the external rites of the sacerdotal ministry and the special sanctification which is their fruit in the interior life of the ministering priest. There would, however, be a great difference in this, that the spiritualizing influence of priestly duties depends much more largely and fundamentally than the grace of the Sacraments, on the personal disposition of the priest himself. The greater his attention to the letter and spirit of the rites and ceremonies pertaining to his role as official minister of God, the greater also will be the richness and fullness of their effect on his own personal life.

If this is so for all priestly functions in general, it is verified in a most perfect manner in the celebration of Holy Mass. Here, where he is privileged to offer the very sacrifice of Christ Himself, the priest reaches the apex of his sacred functions. Certainly, nothing can be better suited than the sacrifice of the Man-God to "draw the priest away from evil and elevate him to a plane of nobility." Hence the priest at the altar should be dominated by the lively conviction that this offering held in his anointed hands is the oblation of Christ Himself. That is why, as St. Cyprian observes, we make mention of our Lord's passion in every Holy Sacrifice which we celebrate. "For," he continues, "this sacrifice which we offer is the passion of the Lord."[3]

In this "heavenly sacrifice," as it is termed by Pope

St. Siricius,[4] we have a continued imitation, or rather a reproduction, of the sacrifice of our Saviour on the Cross. This matchless dignity of the Mass makes it the greatest act which can be performed by man, and, in the language of St. Gregory, the altar of sacrifice becomes the meeting place of heaven and earth:

"Because we see that this present world is already on the decline, we should turn our backs on it and present to God daily sacrifices of tears and the daily oblation of His Body and Blood. This incomparable Victim saves our souls from eternal death and reproduces for us in mystical fashion the death of the only-begotten Son of God. For although through His Resurrection He no longer dies and death will have no more power over Him,[5] nevertheless while living immortally and incorruptibly in Himself, He is once again immolated for us in this mysterious sacred offering. There His Body is received, His flesh is distributed for the salvation of the people, and His Blood no longer stains the hands of unbelievers but rather purples the lips of the faithful.

"Hence let us weigh well what manner of sacrifice this is which is offered for us, and which is a ceaseless imitation of the passion of the only Son of God, to free us from our sins. For who can doubt but that, at the sound of the priest's voice at the hour of sacrifice, the heavens are opened, the choirs of angels stand in reverent awe before the mystery of Jesus Christ, the heights bend down to the depths, earth meets heaven, and the worlds of the seen and the unseen blend into one."[6]

Besides being the offering of the Man-God, the Mass is likewise, in a mysterious manner, the sacrifice of the Church. The complete Christ, St. Augustine never tires of repeating, is not Christ alone nor the Church alone; it is neither the Head nor the members by themselves, but rather the Head with the members — Christ with the Church. Consequently, if the Sacrifice of the Mass is the oblation of the "whole Christ," it must necessarily be in some manner the sacrifice of the Church. From her close association with Christ in His Sacrifice the Church learns from her Divine Spouse how to offer herself with Him and through Him. That is why St. Augustine observes: "Hence the true Mediator took on the form of a servant and became the Mediator of God and man, the Man Christ Jesus. And although as God He shares with the Father the right to receive sacrifice, because He is one God with the Father, nevertheless, as a servant, He preferred to be a sacrifice rather than to accept sacrifice, lest man should be led to think that sacrifice could be offered to creatures.

"It is this which makes Him priest, offerer and offering. And it was His will to make the daily sacrifice of His Church a symbol of this great truth. For since the Church is the Body of which Christ is the Head, the Church learns through Him how to offer herself in sacrifice to God."[7]

If the priest at the altar, as the official representative of the Church, speaks in the name and in the person of Christ, and if in the Mass both Christ and the Church are offered to the Eternal Father, it is not difficult to conclude that the priest must become a spiritual sacrifice in the celebration of Holy Mass. This special duty flows from the very fact of his priesthood, which makes him the representative of Christ, and lays upon him the obligation of doing whatever Christ Himself did. St. Cyprian writes: "For if we are priests of God and Christ, I can find no better model for us to follow than God and Christ, especially since our Lord says in the Gospel: 'I am the Light of the world. He who follows Me does not walk in darkness, but will have the light of life.'"[8]

Elsewhere this same saint makes a more particular application to the priest as being both offerer and offering in the Mass: "If Jesus Christ, our Lord and God, is the High Priest of God the Father, and was the first to offer Himself in sacrifice to the Father, while commanding this same sacrifice to be offered in commemoration of Himself, then that priest really acts in the name of Christ who reproduces in His own life what Christ did for him. He offers a full and perfect sacrifice in the Church to God the Father if he offers his own sacrifice in the same way that he knows Christ offered His."[9]

In a letter which he wrote to Pope St. Cornelius in the name of the II Council of Carthage, St. Cyprian remarks that one of the chief duties of the priest is to prepare victims and offerings for God. He deduces this obligation from the fact of the daily celebration of the Holy Sacrifice of the Mass: ". . . in order that we priests, who daily offer sacrifice to God, may prepare holocausts and victims to the Father."[10]

It is evident from the context of this quotation that the saint here refers to the priest's duty of training and forming the faithful to face the rigors of martyrdom. But it is equally evident that those Christians who were cited before the pagan judges to render an account of their faith were found worthy of martyrs' crowns only because they had previously, through the Mass, made themselves victims of sacrifice with and through their Lord. Hence if one of the priest's most sacred tasks is to teach his people to become living, spiritual sacrifices through their participation in the Mass, he must first master this divine lesson himself by living the sacrifice which it is his daily privilege to offer. In fact, when St. Gregory the Great wished to sum up the edifying life of St. Saturninus, Bishop of Narni, he wrote of him that "he was accustomed to offer daily sacrifice to God, and while giving himself over completely to the sacred mystery of the Mass, he immolated himself with a sacrifice of tears."[11]

From this particular incident in the life of St. Saturninus, St. Gregory passes later to the formulation of a principle of conduct for all priests: "While we are engaged in this mystery, we must immolate ourselves to God in contrition of heart, because when we celebrate the mysteries of our Lord's passion, we must imitate what we do. For He will in all truth be for us a victim before God, if we make ourselves victims before Him."[12]

From these considerations on the interior sentiments which should animate the priest as he offers the Holy Sacrifice, it is not difficult to pass to the thought of the dignity and reverence with which he should be filled as he performs the sacred rites which enshrine the celebration of this august mystery.

Plutarch narrates in his life of the celebrated Roman general, Aemilius Paulus, that after a brilliant military career he was appointed to the sacred office of "augur," or seer, in the city of Rome. In this position it was his duty to take the auspices and to study the portents which appeared to be connected with the welfare of the city. The historian observes how Aemilius Paulus was so devoted to the observance of the traditional rites of his office as to show in his conduct that the priesthood, which meant no more to many men than a stepping-stone to power and riches, was for him really one of the noblest of human professions. In this way, we are told, he became a living proof of the philosopher's definition which states that piety is "the science of the right worship of the divinity."

In consequence of this noble attitude he laid aside all other occupations and set himself to study all the ceremonies connected with his holy position. He was particularly scrupulous to avoid all innovations, changes, or omissions. To those who found fault with his exactitude in small details he replied that it was his duty to be precise, not only as a mark of reverence to the gods, but also out of love for the state. For, he explained, any departure from an order which has been established by law or custom must necessarily and ultimately prove detrimental to the common good.[13]

The application of these reflections of the Roman

seer to the rubrics of the Mass is too evident to require comment. Of course, it would be an exaggeration to page through the Fathers for explicit exhortations to faithful observance of the rubrics. Precise and detailed rubrics, as we know them today, did not appear in the various liturgical books of the Church until centuries after the close of the patristic era. But although they were not acquainted with the term "rubric" in the ecclesiastical and liturgical sense, the Fathers have clearly indicated the dignity and decorum which should characterize the priest at the altar. The foundation of this reverence for the liturgy is explained by St. Leo the Great, when he points out the sacred origin of all the practices of the Church: "There can be no doubt, dearly beloved, but that all the practices of the Christian religion are the result of divine inspiration. Whatever has been adopted into the usages of the Church has come down to us from apostolic tradition and belongs to the teaching of the Holy Ghost. This same Holy Ghost now presides over the hearts of His faithful with His prescriptions so that everyone may keep them in all obedience and wisdom."[14]

In the following exhortation which St. John Chrysostom addressed to the simple faithful we can easily deduce, from the demeanor which he demands of them, the care and dignity to be evidenced by the celebrant of the sacrifice at which they are only to assist with such reverential awe: "Since on this very night our crucified Lord is to appear before us in the guise of a lamb immolated and offered in sacrifice, let us draw nigh to Him, I beg of you, penetrated with lively fear, holy respect, and deep piety. Do you not recall the attitude of the angels at the empty tomb of Christ? Simply because this grave had sheltered His sacred remains, their demeanor was one of deepest respect. Thus the angels, who are far superior to men by nature, manifested before the tomb all piety and respect. Shall we, who are not gathering around an empty tomb, but rather taking our places at the altar whereon the Lamb is immolated, do this amidst noise and confusion?"[15]

With this background it is easy to imagine with what zeal and attention the Fathers conformed to the rubrics prescribed by the Church for the celebration of Holy Mass. Because they went beyond the mere letter of what a modern spiritual writer has so aptly termed "the rules of divine etiquette,"[16] they found therein a source of sanctification which revealed itself to the inquiring eye of faith.

In his letter to Heliodorus on the death of Nepotian, St. Jerome singles out attention to the details of liturgical worship as one of the admirable characteristics of Nepotian's priestly life: "He was always careful to see that the altar was spotless, the walls clean, and the floor well swept. He saw to it that the doorkeeper was at his post and that the curtains were properly hung at the entrance to the church. He made sure that the sacristy was in good order, and the sacred vessels well polished. He manifested a loving care for all the ceremonies of the liturgy, and in this way paid as much attention to the little details as to those of greater importance."[17]

We have another indication of this reverential awe for the ceremonies of the Mass in a passage from a sermon which is attributed to St. Augustine. Here we find a scathing denunciation of an abuse which was even then making its appearance and which has been in recent times stigmatized as the "streamlined Mass." "There is still another point which is most deplorable and on which I cannot refrain from sharing my sorrow with you. It is the fact that there are certain individuals, especially among the more influential persons of the world, who, when they come to church, are not intent on offering praise to God. On the contrary they oblige the priest to shorten the Mass, and to stop the singing whenever they wish.

"As a consequence, the priest is unable to follow faithfully the customs of the Church in the celebration of Mass, and this because of their gluttony and lust for money. For they devote a few moments of their day to their duties to God, and the rest of the day and all of the night to the satisfaction of their own pleasures."[18]

Although it is lamentable when the celebration of the Holy Sacrifice becomes slipshod because of the pressure of external circumstances, it is far less excusable when shoddiness and haphazardness at the altar are due to personal carelessness, nonchalance, or the dwindling faith of the celebrant. Besides the sorrow caused to the angels around the altar by his irreverence, such a celebrant is guilty also of scandal to the faithful and exposes himself to the searing question of Tertullian: *"Sacrificat an insultat?* — Is this priest offering sacrifice to God, or trying to insult Him?"

In conclusion it might be said that the perfect attitude for the priest at the altar is summed up by Lactantius when he describes for the faithful in general the ideal worship of God: "The perfect way to honor God is through direct praise from the mouth of the just man. But if this praise is to be acceptable to God it must be accompanied by humility and reverence and by the greatest possible devotion. This is necessary lest anyone by overconfidence in his sinlessness and innocence be guilty of pride and arrogance and thereby lose the grace that goes with virtue. But in order that a man may be dear to God and be without stain, he should always be begging the mercy of God and plead for nothing else but the forgiveness of his sins.

"Lastly, he should always have God in a consecrated corner of his heart, for he is a temple of God. If he serves God, his Father and Lord, with this constancy, this reverence, and this devotion, then he is practising consummate and perfect justice. And if he perseveres in this perfect service, as we have shown elsewhere, he will obey God and will satisfy the claims of religion and his own obligations."[19]

In these lines of Lactantius we have a description of the Christian who, in his own humble way, renders honor to God after the example of the Divine Master. The priest can have no better model at the altar. Cardinal Mercier, consequently, was speaking in the spirit of the Fathers when he wrote to his seminarians toward the end of his life: "Always offer the Holy Sacrifice as if you were yourselves present at Calvary. Do this with the most fervent faith and devotion of which you are capable. Remember that you became priests in order to offer the Holy Sacrifice." And a young lay college student did not, perhaps, realize the profound significance of a suggestion he made for the further deepening of Christian life at his school: "Have priests say Mass like our Lord would."

PART II

THE PRIEST AND THE PEOPLE

Chapter IV

The Priest's Responsibility for Others

THE priest lives and works for men and their salvation. His special rôle in human life demands a spirit of supreme selflessness and unstinting devotion to others. It summons him to be "all things to all men," because he became a minister of the sanctuary precisely for the salvation and sanctification of others. His office as priest is not personal but primarily and essentially social. Just as the Son of God became man in order to unfold the riches of the Father,[1] so the priest lives his life that he may reveal the life-mysteries of the Son. That is why, as St. John Chrysostom points out, St. Paul spoke of Christ being revealed in him, to the end that he might spend his life in announcing Christ to the nations.[2]

This life of self-sacrificing devotion to others entails many satisfying consolations. The joy of the shepherd over the return of the lost sheep, the exultation of the poor widow at finding her lost groat, the joy of the angels over one sinner doing penance — all these are reflected many times over in the life of the priest. Yet he cannot forget that his responsibility for others will inevitably bring him new troubles and temptations. Reflecting on the worries and anxieties of his own personal life hidden away in the wild fastness of Clairvaux, St. Bernard asks himself what must be the life of a bishop, the priest par excellence, whose duties to souls make him a leader in the Church's struggle against the powers of hell:

"If, I say, the life of every man is a temptation on earth,[3] how many more dangers beset the life of a bishop, who must take upon himself the temptations of his entire flock? If even I, hidden away in a cave and, as it were, under a bushel, not as a shining light but as a smoking wick, cannot withstand the rushing winds but am worn out by the constant assaults of temptation and am blown from side to side like a reed shaken by the wind, what will be the life of him who is set upon a mountain and placed upon a candlestick? . . . With what worries and troubles will not he be beset who, though he may have peace in his own soul, will never be spared from battles without and fears within arising from the lives of others?"[4]

What makes this aspect of his life almost discouraging is that these dangers will inevitably increase according as the priest's zeal widens the field of his selfless devotion to others. Every new conquest for souls leaves him more exposed to the dangers which the devil will undoubtedly throw across his path. Misunderstandings, willful or otherwise, criticism, faultfinding and countless other hardships will beset him continually in an attempt to nullify his efforts or to discourage his zeal. St. John Chrysostom observes: "When I speak of the hardships of the priest's life I am not referring to those who succeed by favoritism, who are seeking only an easy life and looking for a sinecure in the priesthood. I do not refer to them. I speak of those who keep careful watch over your souls, who are more interested in the welfare of their subordinates than in their own ease and comfort.

"Take the case of the father, for example, with ten children who are always in the house and under his control. Even when they are at home, he cannot take his eyes off of them for an instant. But what shall we say of the father whose family is incomparably larger, lives in different houses, and is not in close contact with his authority? You will tell me that he is surrounded with honor. What honor, I ask. The beggars from the crossroads go crying after him wherever he goes. Why does he not silence them, you will ask. All well and good, but that is not the proper thing for a bishop to do.

"Then again, if he is not at the beck and call of everyone, of the unemployed as well as of those who have work, then he will hear a thousand complaints from all sides; everyone presumes to pass judgment on him. Those who hold civil power are protected by the fear which their subjects have for them. It is different with the priest, for there are few persons who are concerned with the fear of God.

"It is impossible to enumerate all the worries that are entailed in preaching and in the duty of teaching. . . . Hence the soul of the priest is like a ship tossed about by the waves; it is assailed from all sides, by enemies and friends, by relatives and strangers. . . . If he manifests emotions he is accused of tyranny; if he uses moderation he is called a weakling. His life consists in reconciling the two extremes of leaving himself open to neither hatred nor contempt."[5]

It is precisely this constant duty of devotion to others which differentiates the priest from the layman or from the simple religious who is not a priest. There is no need to insist that everyone, priest, religious, or layman, is bound by the divine precept of fraternal charity; no one can be dispensed from the fundamental Christian commandment of loving his neighbor. Nevertheless not every walk of life makes a definite profession of devoting itself expressly to the temporal welfare and eternal salvation of others. It is the prerogative of the Catholic priest to be "ordained for men in the things pertaining to God."[6] Thus St. John Chrysostom, addressing an imaginary member of the laity, points out graphically this main difference between the priest and his subjects: "In your case, my dear brother, you are busy about your own affairs and if they move along as they should, you are little concerned about others. Not so with the priest. Even though his life may be altogether blameless, he will be plunged into hell along with sinners if he has not taken a zealous interest in you and in all those who have been entrusted to him. Not infrequently he will be free of all sin himself, and yet he may be lost for not having worked as zealously as he could to prevent sin in others. . . . 'For they keep watch over you' says St. Paul, not in a haphazard or half-hearted way, but 'as having to render an account of your souls.' "[7]

This responsibility for others is not vague and intangible. It is real and concrete. It is a responsibility which will figure in the day of judgment. For if the simple Christian, as we are told by St. Matthew in his description of the Last Judgment, will be judged worthy of heaven or of hell on the basis of what he has done or omitted for the welfare of his neighbors, the same norm will be applied with even more exacting rigor to those whose vocation obliges them to spend themselves and to be spent in the service of their fellow-men. St. John Chrysostom asks: "How shall we bear up under the punishments of the life to come when we shall be called to account for each one of those entrusted to our care? This chastisement will not consist merely of shame, but will be followed by unending punishment. I have already quoted the words of the Apostle: 'Obey your superiors and be subject to them, for they keep watch as having to render an account for your souls.'[8] I must remark here that this threat often echoes in the depths of my soul and fills me with terror. If it is true that to scandalize the least of one's brethren is a greater evil than to be cast into the sea with a millstone around one's neck,[9] and that to wound the weak conscience of one's neighbor is an attack on Christ Himself,[10] what punishment will be meted out to those who cause the loss, not of one, two, or three individuals, but of a whole people?

"It will be to no avail to plead one's lack of ability, to take shelter behind ignorance and to object that ordination was received by force of necessity. If such reasons were legitimate they should be on the lips of subordinates to excuse their own faults, rather than on those of their spiritual leader to cover over the sins of others. Why? Because he whose mission it is to enlighten minds, to announce the approach of the enemy and of the prince of darkness cannot possibly allege ignorance in his own defense. He cannot plead: 'I did not hear the trumpet! I did not expect a battle!' Was he not at his post, as Ezechiel says, precisely to sound the alarm and to announce the coming fray?[11]

"Consequently, he cannot expect to escape punishment even if only one man is thereby lost. We must understand the language of the Lord: 'If, when the enemy advances, the priest does not sound the trumpet to warn the people; if from his watch-tower he does not shout the alarm, and as a result even one person is cut down by the advancing enemy, it may very well be that the victim deserved the lot which befell him. Yet I will require his blood at the hand of this unfaithful watchman.' "[12]

No wonder, then, that St. Augustine could assure his people that they were always "the great preoccupation" of his heart:

. . . "cum cordis nostri negotium semper sitis."[13]

The priest's interest and devotion extend to all the members of his flock. Still, if there is one element of his flock which deserves special care and attention it is that portion which comprises the wayward chil-

dren of the family of God. The first Priest of the New
Law had come, not to save the just, but to call sinners
to repentance; He proclaimed that those who were
well needed not the physician, but rather those who
were sick. To emphasize this aspect of His saving mission, the Saviour of the world gave so much time to
the poor wandering children of Israel that He was
contemptuously called "the friend of publicans and
sinners." Closely allied with these unfortunates in the
attention and care which they should receive are those
who are as yet outside the fold of the one, true Church.
The importance which they should have in the eyes
of their bishops and priests has been embodied in the
Code of Canon Law, which prescribes as a matter of
obligation, not merely of counsel, that all Ordinaries
and pastors shall regard non-Catholics residing within
the limits of their jurisdiction as "entrusted to them
in the Lord."[14] The proper attitude for the priest in
regard to these separated brethren was described very
well by St. John Chrysostom: "There should be no
limit to the priest's efforts to bring back separated
brethren to the unity of the Church. Sheep follow
their shepherd wherever he leads them. If he sees some
stray away from the flock, leave rich pasture-land and
seek in vain for grass among the rocks, he needs only
to shout in order to bring them back.

"But when a man has wandered from the faith,
the pastor has a serious task before him, one which
allows no limit to patience and persevering zeal. It
is neither by force nor by fear, but rather by the power
of persuasion that he will bring back the stray sheep

to the fold of truth. Consequently, he is in need of a noble and generous soul, in order that he may never weaken and never despair of finding and saving the lost sheep."[15]

Since the priest must accommodate himself in all things to the needs and capacity of those over whom he is placed, his strategy in the apostolate must be adapted to circumstances and to individual exigencies. He cannot expect to carry on his priestly work with one hard and fast program or method of action. In this regard the following extract from St. John Chrysostom is so practical and concrete that it could have been written for the busy pastor of today:

"We cannot be satisfied with being ready for only one type of warfare. The war in which we are engaged has many aspects and different enemies are maneuvering against us from different sides. Not all of them attack with the same weapons; they do not all adopt the same tactics. Consequently, the priest who must battle single-handed against so many different enemies must be well-versed in all their changing stratagems.

"At one and the same time he must be slinger and bowman, division and company commander, soldier and general, infantryman and cavalryman, equally skilled in warfare on land and at sea. In ordinary battles each soldier drives off the enemy merely by holding fast the post assigned to him. It is different for us. If we want to win, we must be trained in all manner of warfare; one single weak point in our defense is enough to let the devil push his legions through and plunder the sheepfold. But as soon as he understands that the

shepherd knows all his stratagems and can hold his
own against them, he is stopped in confusion.

"Hence our obligation to be well fortified in all
details. A city completely surrounded by strong ramparts can scoff at its attackers, because it rests in perfect
safety. But if the enemy succeeds in breaking through
a section of the walls, even though the opening be no
wider than a door, the rest of the city's fortifications
are worse than useless.

"It is the same with the City of God. When it has
as its ramparts a watchful and prudent priest, all the
maneuverings of the enemy serve only to increase
his own confusion; the citizens of God mock at these
attacks and suffer no harm thereby. But if there be
a break-through in one sector, if the walls are scaled
at only one point, the whole city is as good as lost.
What is the use of being invincible against the pagans
if we crack under the attacks of the Jews? What profit
is there in vanquishing both pagans and Jews if we fall
into the ambushes of the Manichaeans, or in routing
the Manichaeans if in the meantime the Fatalists succeed in ravaging the flock of Jesus Christ?"[16]

In these words St. John Chrysostom stresses the
need of the priest's readiness to meet all the needs of
his people. With the same ideal in mind he describes
how this readiness manifests itself in action, as the
pastor exercises his office as Mediator by his untiring
service: "You will ask: 'How does the priest plead
my cause before God?' I answer: 'By praying for you;
by giving you the spiritual gift of baptism; by visiting
you; by his generosity in encouraging and advising

you; by coming to your side whenever you call him, even in the middle of the night. In other words, the priest is always ready to help you, even when you give him nothing but disrespect and insults in return.' ''[17]

Hence we can understand how appropriately the Byzantine liturgy for the consecration of a Bishop asks in one of its venerable prayers precisely for this grace of selfless service of others: "Do Thou, O Lord, make this Thy servant to be an imitator of Thee, the true Shepherd, who didst lay down Thy life for Thy sheep; to be a leader of the blind, a light to those who are in darkness, an instructor of the unwise, a teacher of the young, a lamp to the world; that, having perfected the souls entrusted to him in the present life, he may stand unashamed before Thy throne and receive the great reward which Thou hast prepared for those who have contended valiantly for the preaching of the Gospel."

At the same time we get a clearer insight into the appropriateness of the words in which St. John Chrysostom pictures St. Paul explaining the aim of his priestly ministry:

"My aim is not my own glory, nor the splendor of honors and renown. My sole desire is to make the oblation of the Gentiles pleasing to God and sanctified in the Holy Spirit. It is my prayer that the souls of my fellow men will find favor before the Lord. This mission has not been entrusted to me in order to bring honor to myself, but solely to secure your welfare."[18]

Chapter V

Priestly Zeal

THE priest's responsibility for others demands that he be a man of zeal. It is in the exercise of this virtue that he fulfills his obligation of working for others. It has already been remarked that the standard of eternal judgment for even the simple Christian will be his practice of the corporal works of mercy. Consequently, as the Fathers point out, the priest will inevitably be judged according to his measure of zeal in procuring the salvation of those entrusted to him. This is the tremendous thought that inspires St. Gregory the Great:

"Let us picture to ourselves that dread day of reckoning when the Judge will come to exact of us His servants a strict account of our talents. Behold, He will be seen in terrible majesty amid the choirs of angels and archangels. At that moment of terrible scrutiny the entire multitude of the elect and the reprobate will be assembled and each one will be called upon to give an account of his deeds.

"There we shall see Paul, bringing with him the whole of the converted world. Andrew will bring Achaja; John, Asia; and Thomas, India, into the sight of their King. On that day all the leaders of the flock of the Lord will appear with the souls they have won, because by their holy preaching they are bringing to God the flock entrusted to them.

"Consequently, when all these great shepherds appear before the Great Shepherd with their flocks, what are we miserable wretches to say — we who come back to our Lord empty-handed from our mission, we who were called shepherds and who yet have no sheep to show as the result of our efforts? Here we are called 'shepherds,' and there we have no flock to present to God."[1]

Zeal manifests itself visibly in external activity for others. But although its most noticeable manifestations are on the exterior, its roots are sunk deep in the priest's love of God. As has well been said: "Zeal is the overflow of the love of God and our neighbor in a heart which lives by faith." With his usual taste for allegory, St. Gregory the Great draws this important truth from the twice-dyed humeral veil which was among the vestments of the High Priest in his temple functions: "Because it consists in the love of both God and neighbor, the charity of the priest shines, as it were, with a double hue. Consequently, whoever strives after the likeness of his Maker in such a way as to lose interest in his neighbors, or who is so taken up with the care of others as to grow languid in divine love, and thus neglects either one of these two duties, omits to have twice-dyed crimson for the adornment of his superhumeral."[2]

The inspiration of all genuine zeal is in God. No

priest ever engages in the apostolate except to bring men to a greater knowledge and love of their Creator. His activities will unavoidably bring him into the public eye, and gain for him some recognition. Yet even this is referred back to God when the priest is mindful of his proper place in the divine plan of winning souls. In all his activity the Christ-like priest remembers that he is not working for himself but for God. He is mindful with St. Paul that if he pleases men unduly, then he is not a true servant of Christ. Since this is a pitfall to which even many good priests may unconsciously be exposed, St. Gregory devotes almost an entire chapter of his *Regulae Pastoralis Liber* to an eloquent warning against it. He says in part: "In the midst of all this, the pastor must be carefully on his guard lest he be unduly influenced by the desire to please men, and lest in his dutiful attention to interior things and his prudent handling of external business he should seek to draw more love to himself than to truth. Also he must take care lest when he seems sinless to the world because of his good works, self-love should on that account estrange him from his Maker. For whosoever uses his good works to draw the love of the Church to himself instead of to his Lord is an enemy of his Redeemer, and the servant through whom the bridegroom sends gifts to the bride is guilty of adulterous desire if he himself tries to win the affection of the bride."[3]

This zeal for souls is a natural outgrowth of faith in the divinity of Christ. Through the apostolate the priest teaches the people the unsearchable riches of

Christ. He feeds their minds with right doctrine lest they be turned away from the true knowledge of God. His instinctive spirit of conquest for God is aroused by the opportunity to cooperate with the Man-God drawing all things to Himself. Under the inspiration of this deep faith in the divinity of his Saviour, as St. Augustine points out, he feels himself spurred on to share in Christ's eternal battle against the Evil One:

"Those spiritual-minded men who were not satisfied with merely reading in the Gospels about the divinity of our Lord Jesus Christ, felt themselves under the necessity of pitting the arms of Christ against the arms of the devil. Likewise they felt urged to come out in open combat against false and lying teachings on the divinity of Christ lest, through their silence, others should perish."[4]

When participation in the apostolate is thus regarded as a by-product of the spirit of faith, the fact that it is a sacred duty for every priest becomes more convincingly clear. In fact, as St. Gregory remarks, it is precisely by this gift of himself to his fellow men that the faithful priest deepens his likeness to the Son of God: "There are some individuals who have been favored with unusual gifts. But while they restrict their desires to the pursuit of contemplation they shrink away from promoting the welfare of their neighbors through their preaching; they love only the silence of retirement and yearn after the solitude of speculation.

"If we pass strict judgment on these individuals, we

must say that they are guilty of harming as many persons as they could have helped by making themselves servants of the public. What can be the mentality of the man who would be in a position to help others, but who prefers his own solitude to the welfare of his neighbor, when we know that in order to help many, the only-begotten Son of the Eternal Father came from the bosom of the Father into the public eye?"[5]

Because he busies himself with God's work in the apostolate, the zealous priest is protected by divine grace against the spiritual contagion to which he will certainly be exposed. God can never permit work which is undertaken out of love of Him to turn to the spiritual detriment of His apostle. In this way the zealous priest finds in God both his inspiration and his strength. This is the assurance of St. Gregory the Great: "Those priests who give themselves patiently and devotedly to the work of hearing the confessions of their neighbors present the basin of purification at the doors of the temple, in order that whosoever wishes to enter within the gate of eternity may confess his temptations to his pastor, and thus wash the hands of his thoughts and acts in the basin held by oxen.[6]

"It often happens that when devotion to duty brings the mind of the pastor into contact with the difficulties of others, he himself is disturbed by having to listen to these accounts, since the water which purifies the multitude of the people cannot help becoming polluted. And while he takes upon himself the filth of those who are washed, he loses the perfection of his own spotlessness.

"But the pastor should have no fear on this account. For in the inscrutable designs of God, he will be protected all the more easily from his own temptations, in proportion as his greater sympathy for others fatigues and weakens him through the recital of their troubles."[7]

This assurance of God's help, however, does not dispense the priest from realizing his own inability to do God's work by himself; he, too, must ask if he expects to receive. This lays upon him the sacred duty of setting all his activity in the background of a spirit of prayer. According to his usual custom, St. Gregory the Great searches out figures in the Old Testament, and finds in Moses and his attitude toward the Tabernacle of God a perfect model of the zealous priest of the New Law: "Hence it was that Moses frequently went in and out of the Tabernacle, and although within the Tabernacle he was rapt in contemplation still outside it he was beset with the troubles of the weak. Inside he beheld the secret things of God; outside he bore with the burdens of the worldly. In moments of doubt he always had recourse to the Tabernacle, and before the Ark of the Covenant he consulted the Lord. In all this he gave a clear example to pastors that when they are in doubt as to a decision to be taken, they should always enter within themselves as into the Tabernacle, and should consult the Lord before the Ark of the Covenant, when in their doubts they look for light in the pages of Holy Writ.

"For this reason Truth itself, who became visible to us by taking on our human nature, gave Himself to prayer on the mountain-top and worked miracles in the towns below.[8] In this He left an example for good pastors, that, even though they may desire high contemplation, still they must show compassion and companionship with the troubles of the weak. His spirit of love will take him to marvelous heights, when he has first gone down to the depths of his neighbors in a spirit of sympathy. And the kindness which he shows in descending to the level of the weak, will gauge the effectiveness of his ascent to the heights."[9]

In the preceding quotation St. Gregory shows how priestly concern for the spiritual background of zeal naturally carries him over into the field of external activity. No priest can come close to God and share in His spirit of love without sharing also in the divine generosity and expansiveness of that love. That is why St. Gregory could write that St. Paul spent himself in gaining souls for Christ because he knew "how to go beyond himself by contemplation, and at the same time to temper the sublimity of his vision by descending to the level of his hearers."[10] It was in this spirit of love of God and neighbor that the same Paul, who was taken up into the third heaven, also wrote for himself the solemn warning: "Woe is me, if I preach not the Gospel!"[11] Thus it was also that the only-begotten Son of God "who is in the bosom of the Father"[12] insisted against those who would detain Him: "To the other towns also I must proclaim the Kingdom of God, for this is why I have been sent."[13]

Precisely because it is a humble reflection of the zeal of Christ Himself, the devotedness of the priest for others can know no limits; its field lies wherever men are to be saved. Like God Himself, the priest wishes all men to be saved and to come to the knowledge of the truth. For this reason the office of the priest was summed up by St. Ambrose when he wrote that "it belongs to the priestly office to do harm to no one and to be desirous of helping everyone; to accomplish this can come only from God."[14]

The apostolate of the priest is to the great and the lowly, to the powerful and the weak. It is his duty to adapt himself to the particular needs of each soul. "Let them mount the heights," wrote St. Augustine, addressing himself to priests, "that they may lift up the great; let them come down into the depths in order to feed the little ones."[15]

St. John Chrysostom declares: "No matter how insignificant or lowly may be the one who appeals to us, no matter how hard and painful may be what he asks, still if he needs our help, then all the difficulties should seem light and easy to bear. God showed us that the soul is worthy of every care and attention when He did not even spare His own Son."[16]

The great risk incurred in any activity which balances between two extremes is the danger of concentrating on either one to the exclusion of the other. For human nature in its present state there is little probability that the exaggerations of priestly zeal will be on the side of prayer and contemplation. Human contacts afford much more immediate satisfaction than that aroused by concentration on prayer and things spiritual. For this reason the priest's zeal must be well measured lest his attention and efforts be entirely absorbed by the external:

"When the mind dwells complacently on many possible undertakings which may excite the admiration of the faithful, it may easily become puffed up, and arouse the anger of the divine Judge, even though it may not go to the extent of external sin. Our Judge is within us; within us also is the standard according to which we shall be judged. Wherefore when we sin in our hearts, what we do internally is hidden from men, but on the testimony of our Divine Judge we are sinners."[17]

Since the sources of our knowledge bind us down to what is external, it is easy to lose sight of the unseen realities which must be the goal of all activity for souls. Such a reversal of values makes apostolic activity an end in itself, instead of a means of bringing souls to God. The priest who permits outside occupations to usurp an undue place in his life makes his activity a hindrance to his people rather than a help. This is the solemn warning of St. Gregory the Great: "When such pastors are undisturbed by outside worries they are miserable and are bored by their lack of activity. They are never better satisfied than when they are overwhelmed with work, and they regard it as a hard task not to be taken up with earthly worries. Thus it happens that while they rejoice in being harassed by the rush of outside business, they forget the interior lessons which they should have taught to others.

"Hence the faithful grow listless, because despite their desire of spiritual progress, they encounter a stumbling-block in the example of this priest. For if the head is not strong, it is useless for the members to be robust. Likewise, in seeking out the enemy it is useless for the army to advance at top speed if the scout points out the wrong path. Under the guidance of such a priest the minds of the people are not uplifted by exhortation and their faults are not corrected. But while their pastor is acting as judge, his flock is left without a shepherd. The faithful cannot see the light of truth, because while the mind of their pastor is intent on earthly cares he is driven along his path by the wind of temptation, and the dust blinds the eyes of the Church."[18]

Then the saint points out how this selfish conduct can have baneful effects on souls: "When this self-love lays hold of a pastor's mind it sometimes makes him harsh. Self-love makes a priest cowardly, because when he sees his people sinning, he dares not correct them, lest they lose their love for him. Sometimes he goes so far under the influence of this self-love that he connives by his flattery in the faults of his subjects which he should have reproved. . . . This is the conduct of the self-centered pastor toward those who he fears may do him harm in their pursuit of temporal glory.

"But in dealing with those who are powerless against them, such priests bear down with the weight of harsh scoldings and never correct them kindly. Quite the contrary, they forget their duty of pastoral sweetness, and frighten their subjects with the power of authority. . . . Loving themselves more than their Creator, they are haughty toward their subordinates and are less concerned with the abilities of their flock than with showing their own power.

"It must be borne in mind, then, that good pastors should try to find favor with men, but in such wise that by the sweetness of their reputation they may draw their neighbors to a love of truth. They should not desire to be loved for their own sakes, but only in order to make of their love a path along which they may lead the hearts of their listeners to the love of their Creator."[19]

Classical heights on the necessary and close relationship between fruitful zeal and the interior life were reached by St. Bernard of Clairvaux in his celebrated treatise *De Consideratione,* addressed to Pope Eugenius III. Perhaps no one before, and certainly no one since, has synthesized so graphically and with such convincing clarity the fundamental principle of spiritual self-preservation. With the holy liberty born of his former intimacy with Pope Eugenius, and with confidence in the humility evidenced by the Holy Father's filial trust in his former superior, St. Bernard speaks from the depths of his heart and shows how even the office of Sovereign Pontiff can be a source of spiritual ruin: "If you devote your whole life and all your knowledge to activity and nothing to meditation, can I praise you? In this I praise you not. It is not even a good thing for your activity not to be preceded by meditation. If you want to be completely at the service of everyone, after the example of him who became all things to all men, indeed I praise your charity, provided it is really all-embracing. And how can it be all-embracing if it leaves you out? You are a man like all the others to whom you devote yourself. If your charity is to be complete and all-embracing, let the refuge of your heart, which is open to everyone else, find room for you also. Otherwise, as our Lord said, what have you gained if you save everybody else and yet lose yourself?

"Consequently, since you are the property of everyone, try to be one of your own owners. Why should you alone be defrauded of the gift of yourself? You are under obligation to the wise and the foolish, to the rich and the poor, to men and women, to the old and the young — and will you refuse yourself only to yourself? The clergy and the laity, the just man and the sinner — all have a share in what you offer. They all drink from your heart as from a public fountain. Will you stand off by yourself, burning with thirst, while others drink?"[20]

The constant service of others, therefore, can easily become so engrossing as even to blind the zealous priest to the risks he is running in forgetting himself. Hence the seriousness of the warning which the Abbot of Clairvaux addresses to Pope Eugenius: "I would not have you be blind to the slavery into which you are daily, although unwittingly, being forced. It is a sign of dullness of heart not to feel that one is being continually harassed. . . . Take heed, therefore, and not only shake off, but even fly from the yoke of terrible slavery which is not only hanging over you but which is even beginning to press upon you in no small degree.

"There is no worse, no heavier or more disgraceful

slavery than that of the Jews. It keeps them in bondage wherever they go. Tell me then, are you more free than they? When are you safe from bother? When are you your own? You are surrounded with noise and excitement; everywhere the yoke of your bondage weighs heavily upon you."[21]

St. Bernard fears that the Pope and other priests who are in continual contact with the outside will gradually be led to spiritual blindness and hardness of heart. Consequently, he writes with the utmost frankness: "I fear that while you despair of coming to the end of your numerous occupations, you may become hard-hearted and thus deprive yourself of that proper sense of salutary discomfort which is so necessary. It would be much more prudent to get away from your occupations even for a short while, than to allow yourself to be caught up by them and to be dragged where you certainly do not wish to go. Where is that? To hardness of heart. Now do not ask what I mean by that. If the very name does not make you tremble, then your heart is already hardened."[22]

This danger of hardness of heart is so unavoidable and at the same time so fatal in its consequences that St. Bernard does not hesitate to advise the Pope to resign his supreme office if he cannot otherwise safeguard his own spiritual welfare.[23] To prove that this danger is not a frightening specter which he has conjured up for mere oratorical effect, he proceeds to sketch with masterly touch the various steps which lead down from the glowing heights of fervor to the cold depths of an unresponsive heart:

"At first some little infidelity will seem to you unbearable. In the course of time, if you make a habit of it, you will regard it as not so serious after all. After a time you will think it is unimportant. Still a little while longer and you will not even notice it. A short time later and you will find pleasure in it. This is the slow but none the less certain path to hardness of heart, and from there it is only a step to positive aversion for what is good."[24]

In the conclusion of the second chapter of Book I *De Consideratione,* the holy abbot allows himself a surprising freedom in qualifying duties which distract a priest from necessary attention to his own sanctification and salvation. In the well-known peroration to the chapter he exclaims in the heat of his fervor: "This is the extreme to which your *cursed occupations* (occupationes maledictae) can lead you, if you continue, as you have begun, to give yourself over to them unreservedly, and leave nothing for yourself."[25]

In the mind of the Fathers, consequently, sacerdotal zeal must be mainly an outward expression of inward love. This almost sacramental significance of priestly devotedness has its roots in God and thence stretches out into the world of souls. The zealous priest deploys all his activity between God and men. His zeal flows from his faith in God which inspires him to want to bring men back to their Lord and Master. From God, too, he draws his strength and courage in prayer.

This nearness to God influences every aspect of priestly activity for souls. Zeal becomes expansive and all-embracing like God's own love for man. Zeal springs from the inspiration of prayer, while the quiet of prayer perfects and ennobles the background of zeal. In this setting the priest balances his zeal perfectly between the two extremes of God and man. Realizing his duties to both, he endeavors to neglect neither. He is aware that in his pastoral life it would be just as wrong to spend all his time in prayer as it would be to devote his entire energy to outside activity. In a word he has an eye both to God and to man, lest, after preaching to others, he himself should be rejected.

Chapter VI

Good Example

THE social responsibility of the priest constitutes him a public personage. Hence he is not at liberty to judge his actions merely in their relationship to himself. Wherever he appears, whether officially or privately, he represents the Church and stands for her ideals. In consequence, he must always bear in mind that whatever he does will redound to the credit or discredit of the priesthood and of the Church at large. It is true that the Church is divine. As the Mystical Body of Christ, she cannot suffer harm in her divine reality. But, like Christ Himself, she can suffer in her members. More particularly, she can suffer in those members who are her ministers. That is why priests may so well apply to themselves the pleading exhortation of St. Ambrose to a group of holy virgins to safeguard in their conduct the good reputation of the Church: "Not in herself, my daughters, not in herself, I say, are wounds inflicted on the Church, but in us. Let us take heed, therefore, lest our fall be a wound in the body of the Church."[1]

This responsibility of representing the Church is

summed up in the priest's all-embracing obligation
of giving good example to the faithful in all the circumstances of life. We might be surprised at the
insistence of the Fathers on this point, did we not
realize with them how closely the exemplary life of
the clergy is bound up with the welfare and prosperity
of the entire Church. As a preface to subsequent quotations emphasizing the sacerdotal duty of edification,
we may consider the following passage from St. Gregory
the Great which depicts the portrait of the ideal
priest:

"The conduct of the pastor should be as far above
the conduct of the people as the life of the shepherd
is above the life of his flock. He should strive to cal-
culate carefully how strictly he is bound to righteousness when, in comparison with him, his people are
called his flock. Consequently, he must be pure in
thought, outstanding in activity, discreet in silence,
helpful in speech, close to everyone through sympathy,
elevated above all others by the practice of contemplation, a companion in humility to those who do
good, firm against evildoers through zeal for justice,
not lessening his solicitude for internal things by
being unduly occupied with those of the outside, and
not neglecting attention to external duties by excessive
concentration on the interior life."[2]

Five centuries later, and perhaps spurred on by the
inspiration of this passage from St. Gregory, St. Bernard develops in realistic detail the thought which
the great Pope has suggested: "If the priest is a shepherd, and the people are sheep, is it right for the

shepherd to be no different from his flock? If like me, who am a sheep, my shepherd walks bent over, with his face cast down and always turned toward the ground hungrily looking only for fodder for his belly, what difference is there between us? Woe is me if the wolf comes. There will be no one to see him, to meet him, or to save the sheep.

"Is it proper for the shepherd, like his sheep, to be intent on his bodily senses, to be attached to debasing things, and to yearn after the things of earth? Is it not more fitting for him to stand upright like a man, to behold the heavens with the eyes of his mind, to seek and savor the things that are above rather than those which are upon the earth?"[3]

St. Gregory has indicated how the faithful look up to their spiritual father as to a model. In characteristically graphic language, St. John Chrysostom explicitly develops this same theme, and points out the manifestly inherent contradiction of preaching one thing and doing another. At the same time he warns priests not to forget that the great dignity with which they are clothed cannot be expected to hide their faults from those over whom they are placed: "Subordinates are accustomed to take their superior for their example and model; they form themselves along the lines which they see in him. If he loses patience easily, how can he calm the impatience of others? What private individual will desire to practice restraint and meekness if he sees his superior in the throes of anger? The faults of priests cannot be hidden; even the slightest of them stands out. As long as an athlete stays at home and engages no opponents, even though he be completely out of condition, yet his weakness is still not known. But just as soon as he prepares for an encounter and descends into the arena, he shows what he is.

"In the same way those who stay by themselves and live in retirement can hide their failings behind the veils of solitude. But if they come out into the open, once they leave their life of retirement and seclusion and cast off the cloak which covered them, they necessarily show forth in their outward conduct the most secret recesses of their heart. Then their virtues are a help to the people by arousing the desire of imitation. But at the same time their faults give rise to spiritual sluggishness and indifference and paralyze good thoughts and good works. The beauty of their soul must shine before the eyes of all in order to enlighten and gladden those who behold it. . . .

"The priest, so to speak, should be clothed in sparkling armor protecting him on all sides. He should keep guard over his own life with untiring zeal and ceaseless vigilance so that it will be impossible to detect a fault in him. For he is always surrounded by snares. At every moment enemies are lying in wait to ambush and wound him. And among his numerous enemies will be found some who advance under the cloak of friendship."[4]

Again St. Gregory would have us find in the priest a man of perfect balance and right proportion. The priest, according to his ideal, must be intent on the things of God while not neglecting the things of men;

he must avoid exaggerated emphasis on both sides of his life lest his erroneous viewpoint should give the Church a bad name, as though she taught her ministers to look down with contempt on the ordinary routine duties of Christian life. For this same reason St. Bernard requires that the priest's conduct never depart from what is reasonable. This does not mean that he is to conform to all the whims and fancies of those around him. Nevertheless, every aspect of his conduct must be grounded so solidly on the fundamental requisites of priestly holiness and so co-ordinated with the exigencies of good judgment, that even those who criticize his viewpoint will be forced to admit that he is right in the light of these basic principles. This is the reserved and prudent conduct which St. Bernard urged upon Pope Eugenius when he pleaded with him to prosecute energetically reform of the papal court at Rome. At the same time he counseled discretion lest objections against the person of the reformer be ultimately directed against the substance of the reform itself. He concluded with the following significant phrase: "They may protest that this or that has never been done before; but they cannot deny that it is right."[5]

That is why St. Gregory says that priests and monks are to be admonished in accordance with the duties peculiar to each one's state in life: "When we see a cleric, he is to be admonished so to comport himself as to give an example of right living to people in the world, lest, if he should show himself blameworthy, his failings should lessen the esteem in which our holy religion is held. And when we see a monk, we should admonish him to be always circumspect in thought, word and deed, and thus in his actions to show reverence for his habit, in order that he may be perfectly detached from the world, and show forth in his conduct before God what he represents to human eyes by his dress."[6]

Unless the priest wishes to waste his time when he preaches, he must exemplify in his own conduct the ideals which he sets forth when teaching. St. Gregory bears out the truth of this observation when he remarks that the teacher who violates a commandment will be called the least in the kingdom of heaven, because if a priest's life does not command respect, the only alternative left is that his preaching will be disregarded.[7] And Cassian recorded the sage observation of a holy hermit to the effect that "the arguments of the preacher will be of no avail unless he has fixed them in the hearts of his listeners with works which show their effect."[8]

St. Gregory has said that the pastor must be outstanding in his activity; the activity to which he chiefly refers is summed up in giving example: "The pastor must be outstanding for his activity, in order that by his conduct he may point out to his subjects their way of life, and in order that by following the voice and the motions of the shepherd the flock may advance more by his example than by his words. For he who is compelled by his position to preach the highest doctrine is by that same necessity constrained to give the highest example. The voice of the preacher penetrates more easily into the hearts of his hearers when it is borne out by his life, since he thus helps them by his example to do what he commands in his sermons."[9]

This has been a favorite theme with all spiritual teachers. St. Ambrose writes that a sermon will be all the more acceptable to the listeners according to the greater holiness of the preacher.[10] St. Augustine in turn insists that the harm done by preachers whose lives are inconsistent with their teaching does not come from the good and holy things which they preach but from the bad example of which they are guilty, "for in so far as the priest acts wrongly, he is not preaching from the chair of Christ."[11]

In his usual roughshod manner, St. Jerome advises Nepotian along the same lines: "Do not permit your actions to belie your words, lest when you preach in church someone should ask himself: 'Why do you not practise what you preach?' He is a poor teacher who preaches fasting with a full stomach. Even a robber can talk eloquently against avarice. In the priest of Christ everything — mouth, mind, and hands — should be in perfect harmony."[12]

With surprising realism the Fathers insist in season and out of season on the perfect co-ordination of priestly life and teaching. Representing in a simile from the physical world the graphic contrast between life and teaching in the careless priest, St. Bernard writes to Pope Eugenius: "It is a spiritual monstrosity to be set in a high place and to have one's soul in the depths; to be first in rank and last in conduct; to be eloquent in speech and lazy at work; to speak much and to do little; to be solemn in expression and frivolous in conduct; to wield immense authority and yet to rest on a tottering foundation. . . .

"Even though this may not be a picture of yourself, nevertheless examine your conscience to see where you have failed, lest you grow complacent in your goodness. I would have you glory in the testimony of a good conscience, and at the same time find in that same testimony food for humility."[13]

Since good example from their spiritual shepherds is so necessary for the normal life of Christ's flock, it follows that the priest who fails in this duty introduces a fatal germ of death into the ministry of supernatural life: "Those who are set over others should bear in mind that for every act of bad example which they pass on to their subjects they are guilty of spiritual murder. Hence they should safeguard themselves all the more carefully against sin, because through the evil which they perpetrate, they not only die themselves, but are also answerable for the souls of others which they have destroyed by their evil conduct."[14]

It is equally evident that the duty of the priest toward his people goes far beyond the merely negative obligation of refraining from disedifying behavior. According to St. Gregory the Great, the very nature of his office requires that he give really positive help to those whose general spiritual welfare and formation have been entrusted to him by God through the Church: "Whoever is appointed to show others how to live, must not only be vigilant himself, but is thereby admonished that he must also arouse his friends. It is not enough for the priest to await the coming of the Lord through a good life, unless at the same time he arouses those under him from the torpor of sin."[15]

This priestly duty of positively helping others is not based on the demands of high and heroic spirituality; it is of the very essence of the sacerdotal office. St. Gregory stresses this point when he assures us that harmony of life and teaching is called for by the simple dictates of reason. Even in merely human circles, he remarks, whoever is not careful to harmonize practice and theory is "entangled in his words and trapped in the snares of speech."[16] This human element comes into play again in the consideration that the faithful are expected to imitate their priests. But, observes St. Augustine, no one can imitate another, if this other is displeasing to him.[17] Nothing, in turn, makes a priest more obnoxious to his people than discrepancy between his preaching and his actions. The result is that the pastor who is not fully intent on good example nullifies his ministry, neutralizes the good which he might otherwise do, and makes it impossible for his people to have the right attitude toward him and his place in their life.

The effects of the bad example of priests on the lives of the faithful are vividly described by St. Gregory when he develops a figure of speech taken from the Prophet Ezechiel:[18] "Shepherds drink clear and sparkling water when, with a right understanding, they draw from the streams of truth. But to stir up this water with one's feet is to ruin the work of meditation by bad example. The sheep drink riled water when they do not follow the advice which they are given. They thirst after what they hear explained to them, but since this is spoiled by evil conduct, they drink muddy water from their springs."[19]

The most regrettable aspect of bad example by priests is the quasi-immunity from reprimand with which their life is surrounded. Because of their dignity as ministers of the Lord they will rarely, if ever, be corrected for their shortcomings. This only aggravates a condition which can already lead to disastrous consequences. St. Gregory sensed this lamentable situation: "No one does more harm in the Church than he who gives bad example and at the same time bears a name and exercises an Order which implies sanctity. No one will presume to correct such a person, and the evil effects of his bad example are made all the worse, when honor must be paid to a sinner because of this reverence which is owed to Holy Orders."[20]

This difficulty is rendered still more difficult and complicated by the permanence of the priestly character. No matter what may be his failings, or even his sins, a priest always remains a priest, and this fact perpetuates the unpleasant circumstances just referred to by St. Gregory. The tepid monk, we are told by Cassian, was immediately deprived of his habit and driven from the monastery.[21] Such drastic measures could not very easily be resorted to with those who have been made priests of the Lord *in aeternum*. The Church must bear with them patiently.

Good and fervent priests, however, who are always more numerous than their unfortunate brethren, have always in mind their great responsibility of maintaining and protecting the good name of the Church. In the words of St. Ambrose, they never forget that whatever good they do will certainly contribute to the honor and glory of their Divine Master: "Thus, in St. Paul's qualifications for the ministry, we see how many qualities are asked of us: that the minister of the Lord should refrain from the use of wine, and be safeguarded by the good testimony, not only of the faithful but also of those outside the fold. It is fitting that the public eye should be witness of our acts and works, lest it lose respect for our office; in order that whoever sees the minister of the altar adorned with fitting virtues should give glory to their Author, and honor the Master who has such servants."[22]

It would be a mistake, however, to think that the danger of disedification of the faithful by the priest is restricted to the field of actual sin. We might even say that this is the field in which least danger is to be expected. The example which is expected of the ministers of the altar deals more particularly with a spirit or attitude of mind than with determined individual actions. It is the general reserve of their conduct and the dignity of their demeanor which constitute the main basis of their influence. Such qualities evidence the perfect co-ordination of their whole lives; as a man is, so does he act. A well-regulated exterior is the surest indication of a well-balanced life. In his *De Officiis Ministrorum* St. Ambrose draws on his own experience for a case in which concern for gravity in external conduct motivated his rejection of a candidate for the

sacred ministry. He points out how this man, along
with another whom he found among his clergy on his
arrival in Milan, later fully justified the misgivings
which the carelessness of their outward bearing inspired: "You will recall, my sons, a certain friend of
yours who appeared to be characterized by a great
devotion to duty. I refused, nevertheless, to admit him
into the ranks of the clergy for this one reason, namely,
that his external comportment was highly unbecoming.
You will also recall that there was a second individual
whom I found already admitted into the clergy, and
that I gave orders that he was never to be with me in
procession, because the very insolence of his walk
struck me across the eyes like a whip. That was my
command when he was reinstated in his functions after
a fall. He is the only one whom I ever treated thus,
and my verdict was not belied by events. Both of these
individuals fell away from the Church, and they thus
gave sufficient proof of the depravity of soul which
they betrayed in their outward demeanor."[23]

Hence it was that the inescapable human element
in priestly contact with souls furnished the Fathers
with countless occasions for insisting on external decorum and dignity, or on what we would today call by
the simple name of "gentlemanliness." We are often
led to believe that the generation of the Fathers was
rough and uncouth, that the niceties of human intercourse were frowned upon as savoring too strongly of
worldliness. Nevertheless we find the Fathers sensing
that the priest must be loved by his people, and they
understood how greatly this affection could be en-

couraged and strengthened if the priest was humanly approachable. St. Ambrose wrote: "We should bear in mind, first of all, that nothing is so useful as to be loved, and that nothing is so useless as not to be loved, for I feel that to be disliked is fatal. Consequently, we ought so to comport ourselves as to build up in all things respect and a good opinion of ourselves.

"In the first place let us attract the affection of men by calmness of mind and kindness of attitude. Goodness finds favor with everyone and there is nothing which so easily wins the hearts of men. If divine grace is seconded by this gentle and easy manner through the moderation of our commands and the affability of our conversation, the dignity of our language and the measured calm and restraint of our discussions, it is almost unbelievable how powerfully all this will contribute to building up love and affection for us."[24]

The meekness, calm, and reserve of conduct which St. Ambrose here recommends so highly to members of the clergy are really nothing more than the perfection of those same qualities which are demanded in every Christian. The grace of Holy Orders will not cover over natural defects of character. This grace may, on the contrary, even make these weaknesses more glaring and prominent in the light of the sanctuary. The priesthood cannot be expected to supply the lack of natural virtues any more than it can compensate for the absence of fundamental Christian virtues. As St. Jerome says with such biting sarcasm: "The mere fact of being a dignitary in the Church will not make you a Christian."[25]

Hence the development of gentlemanly priestly character calls for generous and tireless effort from all who actually are clerics as well as from all who aspire to be of their number. To priests in a very special manner St. Gregory would apply the exhortation which he intended primarily for the simple faithful: "Let us take care, dearly beloved brethren, lest any uncleanness defile us who in the eternal foreknowledge of our Creator have been made citizens of God and the equals of His angels. Let us prove our dignity by our conduct. May no sins of the flesh soil us, no unclean thought point an accusing finger at us, no evil intention gnaw at our mind, no rust of envy eat it away, no honor puff it up, no ambition drag it through the pleasures of earth, and no burst of anger set it on fire. For men have been called gods. Therefore, O man, defend the honor of God against your faults, because for your sake God was made man."[26]

In a word, to sum up all these fundamental truths in a profoundly practical phrase of St. Bernard, every priest should tell himself as the Abbot of Clairvaux told Pope Eugenius: "Either show yourself a shepherd to your people, or cease to claim the title."[27]

And St. Jerome wrote: "The priest of Christ should be so blameless in his conduct that even the critics of religion will be unable to find fault with his life."[28]

Chapter VII

The Use of Authority

THE divine functions of the priesthood entail the exercise of great authority, both in the interior world and in the exterior world. From this consideration, however, it should not be inferred that the minister of Christ may be high-handed and arrogant in using the power of his exalted office. On the contrary, his is the sacred and difficult obligation of reconciling the exercise of almost undisputed authority with deep convictions of humility and reserve. His dignity never entitles him to exaggerate the prerogatives to which his position gives rise. There is no higher dignity in the entire world than that of the Sovereign Pontiff. At the moment he bows to receive the tiara, the Head of the Church is reminded that he is the "Father of princes and kings, Ruler of the visible world, and Vicar of our Lord Jesus Christ." These are titles which no other human being presumes to claim. Yet even in the official exercise of this supreme power the Sovereign Pontiff terms himself "the servant of the servants of God."

Hence it is that the Fathers stress over and over

again the perfect discretion which should characterize the priest's use of authority. As St. Bernard points out, humility is a virtue which always attracts others and wins their hearts. When there is question of persons invested with high authority, the drawing power of humility and discretion is intensified many times over: "Humility is the solid foundation on which the whole spiritual structure is built and grows into a holy temple in the Lord. Through humility some persons have even taken by storm the gates of the enemy. No other virtue is as powerful as humility to vanquish the pride of demons or the tyranny of men. Even though humility is a veritable tower of strength from the force of the enemy, still, somehow or other, its power is more evident in great people, and stands out more clearly in those who are prominent. There is no more sparkling jewel in the whole adornment of the Sovereign Pontiff. For in proportion as he is more exalted than others, he stands out in his humility as being elevated above himself."[1]

If he is to remain well-grounded in humility, the priest can put no trust in the empty praise of men. Flattery will necessarily come his way, but his penetrating spiritual insight makes him see through the futility of it all, and, as St. Bernard remarks so well, enables him to understand that his true glory cannot remain wholly in the power of his fellow men: "It is unsafe to entrust one's glory to the lips of men, which are like a coffer without key or lock, and open to anyone who wishes to break in. It is not only not safe but positively stupid to deposit your treasure where you cannot get it back at will. If you put your treasure in my mouth, it is no longer in your power but in mine, for according to my own whim I can either add to your praise or take away from it."[2]

St. Gregory also points out eloquently how the priest can easily fall into the snare of human adulation: "Seduced by the flattery of inferiors, the mind is puffed up, and while it is externally surrounded with great favor, it is inwardly emptied of the truth. Forgetful of self it relies on what others say, and considers itself to be what reputation proclaims, instead of judging according to internal values. It looks with contempt on its subjects, refuses to recognize them as equals in the order of nature, and because it has risen above them in power, thinks that it has also exceeded them in merit. A man thinks that he knows more than anyone else, simply because he has more authority. He takes his place on some sort of eminence, and although he is bound within the same limits of nature as everyone else, still disdains to regard others as equals."[3]

Because of the esteem and respect which are so generously tendered him, the priest is in an unfortunate situation. Whereas the whole spiritual atmosphere of his life calls for humility, nevertheless everything around him conspires against a humble opinion of himself. From this sad fact St. Gregory draws the sobering lesson that no one will become humble in the priesthood. If the candidate for Holy Orders has not schooled himself thoroughly in humility during those years of closer subjection to authority which mark the period of his formation, he will never change his habits of pride once he attains to a position of ecclesiastical prominence: "Hence it is that when our thoughts go wandering, our mind's eye should be at once directed to our past life. And as each one weighs carefully how he acted as a subject, he will at once see if he will be able in a position of authority to do the good which he has set himself to accomplish. For no one can ever succeed in learning humility in a position of eminence, if he was unable to conquer pride as a subject. And no one can flee from the suggestion of praise when it is present, if he learned to long for it when it was absent."[4]

Consequently, priests who set their hearts on attaining ecclesiastical preferments and dignities really demonstrate that they have no genuine understanding of the office to which they aspire: "Whoever is in search of glory and honor, rather than of an opportunity to do good, is proof against himself that he does not really desire a bishopric. The man who strives after a position of authority, feeds in his inmost thoughts on the satisfaction of having others under him, finds joy in his own praise, yearns for honor and exults in the abundance of prosperity. He not only has no love for the sacred office which he covets, but does not even understand what it is. He is really looking for worldly profit under the guise of that honor whereby worldly gain was to have been destroyed."[5]

It behooves every priest, therefore, to be distrustful of himself when he finds himself desiring positions of authority out of supposedly praiseworthy reasons. On this score St. Gregory appeals to the example of holy men: "Hence let headstrong men understand how blameworthy they are in deliberately desiring to be placed over others, when holy men hesitated to become leaders of their people even at the command of God. Moses trembled at the commission of God, and still many seek honor. Men who are already tottering under the weight of their own burdens, gladly offer their shoulders to carry the loads of others. And although they can hardly put up with what they had before, they still increase their load."[6]

And again: "We have made these brief remarks to show how great is the burden of authority, lest an unfit candidate should rashly take over the reins of power, and through a desire of prominence, lead himself to perdition."[7]

From these serious warnings St. Gregory would not have us gather the erroneous impression that authority is an evil thing in itself. His only purpose is to forestall what might easily become a disastrous danger for an individual priest and even for the entire Church. "In these observations," he says, "we are not condemning power. Still we are endeavoring to strengthen weak hearts against a desire of authority, lest imperfect men should venture to heights of power, and step on the edge of a precipice when they are not steady on their feet even on level ground."[8]

True humility will not allow a priest to shirk positions of authority which are assigned to him by lawful superiors. Notwithstanding his natural repugnance to any such prominence, humility will demand that he acquiesce for the good of the Church: "There are some priests, who, out of humility, shrink from positions to which they feel themselves unequal. And if their humility is linked up with other virtues, then it is genuine in the eyes of God, because it will not be stubborn in refusing what it is commanded to accept.

"It is not true humility, however, to recognize God's will as commanding acceptance of authority and still not to obey. But when a position of power is assigned by superiors to one who has gifts which can be helpful to others, he should submit to the divine plan and, without any trace of obstinacy, he should deep down in his heart shun the position, and yet obey in spite of himself."[9]

In this unwilling acceptance of a position of power, the priest, like Moses, gives evidence of twofold humility: "He [Moses] was doubly humble and doubly obedient; for in his own estimation he was unwilling to lead his people, and yet he trusted in the strength of Him who gave the command, and accepted."[10]

With the background of such sentiments of humble self-distrust the genuine priest will exemplify the truth of what St. John Chrysostom had in mind when he wrote: "The imposition of hands confers no title to power, prominence, or authority. We have all received the same spirit; we have all been called to the adoption of sons. It is the will of the Father that those whom He has chosen for His own should put their dignity at the service of their brethren."[11]

The constant recollection of one's own frailty is provided by the fact that even in positions of authority one's individuality remains unchanged. This furnishes an effective check on any movements of self-love which might be aroused by the thought of successes already obtained: "Although Almighty God often gives greater perfection to the minds of pastors, still not infrequently He leaves them deficient in some respect. This He does in order that, while they shine forth with admirable virtues, they may be mellowed by putting up with their own imperfections, and not be proud over their gifts when they realize that they still have trouble in fighting against little things. Thus, since they cannot get perfect control of those small points, they dare not show pride at their more important actions."[12]

Hence the priest will always fear in himself the possibility of what the duties of his office oblige him to correct in others: "When you become irritated at the frailty of others, remember what you are yourself, in order that you may be moderate in your zeal for correction. You should fear for yourself what you must reprimand in others."[13]

Nor does the fact of one's own weakness remain a mere possibility. Hence, in the words of St. Gregory, the duty of welcoming correction: "There is no one so perfect as not to fail sometimes. Therefore the priest evidences a greater love for truth than for himself if he wants others to be honest in their corrections, even though this frankness may possibly hurt his feelings."[14]

St. John Chrysostom observes how the fact of their own failings and weaknesses is one of the potent means with which priests are provided by God to guard themselves against abuse of authority: "If the teachers and priests of the Church were exempt from sin and worldly passions, they would treat their fellow men without mercy or gentleness. Priests and superiors have been subjected to their passions like everyone else, in order that they may learn from their own trials how to be considerate in dealing with others.

"Such has always been God's way of acting, in the past as in the present. He allowed those to whom He intended to entrust His Church and His people to fall into sin, so that the remembrance of their own lapses might make them more indulgent toward their brethren. Had they never sinned themselves, they would never have any pity for sinners and in the harshness of their judgment they would drive all sinners out of the Church."[15]

In these quotations the Fathers show that the ideal priest must avoid undue severity in the exercise of his authority. At the same time they sense equal danger in the opposite extreme of excessive leniency and mildness. An erroneous concept of humility cannot be allowed to interfere with necessary insistence on pastoral discipline. The self-abasement of the pastor must be such that while his humility edifies his subordinates, his authority remains unimpaired and ready for whatever severity may be necessary: "In all this, care must be taken lest through the excessive practise of humility respect for authority be weakened, and lest while the pastor belittles himself he should lose all power to hold his people under the sway of discipline. In their external conduct, then, pastors should hold fast to the authority which they have received for the welfare of others and, so far as they themselves are concerned, they should be fearful in their own appraisal of themselves."[16]

Hence, observes St. John Chrysostom: "It is of the utmost importance that the teacher should not be made light of. But how can he practise humility and meekness, you will ask, if he is never despised? As far as he himself is concerned, he should bear patiently with whatever disrespect he may encounter; such patience will contribute greatly to the success of his teaching.

"When it is a question of others, however, such a stand would no longer be humility but weakness. If the priest avenges his personal insults or any injuries which may be inflicted on him or the snares which may be laid for him, he does wrong. But as soon as the salvation of your brethren is involved, then command and use all the authority at your disposal. In such a case, reserve would be altogether out of place; the priest must use then all his authority to avert common ruin."[17]

With the full conviction of his dignity thus ever before him and yet without assuming an air of arrogance or despotism, the priest will know how to insist on the reverence to which his divine mission entitles him. This realization will teach him the necessity of prescinding from any of those natural considerations which, humanly speaking, would interfere with the efficiency of his apostolate. If he is to succeed in the spiritual care of the faithful he cannot fall victim to what modern psychologists call an "inferiority complex." No priest could be more self-effacing or more genuinely humble than Chrysostom of Antioch. In fact we know that he had to be forced into the priesthood almost by physical violence. Yet it was this same humble Chrysostom who proclaimed the following energetic vindication of his rights and privileges as priest and bishop: "As long as we occupy this throne, as long as we are in charge, notwithstanding our own unworthiness, we have authority and power. The chair of Moses called forth such admiration that it gave authority to whoever spoke in the name of Moses. How much more true this is when there is question of the chair of Christ! Now it is this chair which we occupy. It is from the heights of this chair that we speak in the name of Christ Himself who has entrusted to us the ministry of reconciliation.

"All ambassadors, whoever they may be, by the mere fact of being ambassadors, enjoy privileges of high distinction. By virtue of these privileges they are entitled to enter enemy territory and to advance unescorted among barbarians. Such is the almost sacred character of every such mission that the most complete respect and the most perfect safety are altogether essential to it.

"Now we, too, have the title of ambassadors, and we come in the name of God. This is the distinguishing mark of the episcopate. We come to you, charged with a mission. Our mission is to beg of you to put an end to all war. As peace terms we do not offer you merely the keys to a few cities, provisions of grain, slaves or gold, but rather the very kingdom of heaven, eternal life, everlasting companionship with Christ, and other untold benefits which tongue cannot describe nor mind imagine as long as we are held in by the bonds of this mortal life.

"That is our mission to you. Hence we intend to take advantage of the privileges which this sacred mission implies. We do this, not because of our own personal worth — we know full well our own unworthiness — but for your sakes. We wish to be assured that you will pay proper attention to our preaching, that you will really profit by it, and that you will not neglect the teaching which we offer to you. You know how ambassadors are everywhere honored. We are God's ambassadors to men. If you think my expressions are exaggerated, then I shall say rather: 'Bishops, not I personally, are God's ambassadors to men — not any particular individual but bishops in general.' Consequently, even though you may not wish to respect my person, at least have reverence for my dignity."[18]

Accordingly the priest cannot follow a principle of universal severity nor a policy of universal leniency. His sense of judgment, writes John Chrysostom, will tell him when he may reasonably allow some points to pass unnoticed, and when it is his duty to react with all the authority of his office: "There are some things which are to be taught and others which need to be prescribed. If you command when you should only teach, you make yourself ridiculous; and the same is true if you only teach when you should command. By this I mean that the obligation to avoid evil is not merely something to be taught but rather something to be ordered with all the weight of one's authority. . . .

"If you are to speak of almsgiving, virginity, or of

the truths of faith, that is the time to teach. Hence St. Paul's twofold injunction: 'Command, teach.' Likewise if someone carries charms and trinkets, knowing full well that this is wrong, that is a case which calls for a command, but if the circumstances are such that he does not know that such a practice is wrong, then the circumstances demand that he be taught. As you see, the priest must know how to command, and how to speak with authority, and not limit himself to merely preaching doctrine."[19]

St. Gregory reverts to this truth very frequently in his portrayal of the ideal priest. With his usual fondness for allegory he finds foundations for comparisons in both the Old and the New Testaments. Speaking of the pedestals in the Temple which were adorned with figures of lions and oxen and surmounted by Cherubim he draws a lesson for those in authority: "What else was signified by the pedestals in the temple, but priests in the Church? While they are beset with the worries of government, they carry a great burden after the manner of pedestals. Rightly, then, are the Cherubim represented on the pedestals, because it is altogether fitting that the heart of the priest should be filled with knowledge.

"Wholesome fear of severity is signified by the lions, and patient meekness by the oxen. Consequently, on these pedestals we find neither the lions without the oxen, nor the oxen without the lions, because the heart of the priest should always keep watch over the rigors of severity with the virtue of meekness, in order that moderation may season his wrath, and that zeal for severity may enkindle this same meekness, lest it lose all its force."[20]

The holy doctor sees this same lesson in the use of both oil and wine by the good Samaritan to dress the wounds of the man who fell among robbers: "The cause of discipline or of mercy is much weakened if either is practiced without the other. In dealing with his subjects the pastor must use both the consolations of gentleness and the rigors of discipline. Hence it is that both wine and oil were used on the wounds of the half-dead man who was taken to the inn by the Samaritan, in order that his wounds might be purified by wine and softened by oil. This shows that all who are charged with healing wounds, should see in wine the sting of severity, and in oil gentle affection; through wine festering cares should be purified, and through oil hastened on the road to recovery.

"In this same way, kindness is to be mingled with severity, and the right combination of both must be applied so that subjects will not be hardened by undue severity, nor grow lax with excessive leniency."[21]

Perfect co-ordination between the demands of personal humility and the exigencies of official authority will give to the faithful many opportunities for respecting the authority of their priests while they imitate their humility. This is a further thought of St. Gregory: "The faithful should find priests practising humility in their personal conduct, so that they may have reasons for respecting their authority and imitating their humility. Let superiors, consequently, be all the more humble in their own eyes according as their external authority is greater, lest it gain control of their mind and carry them off in self-satisfaction, and lest the mind should lose all control over this authority to which the pastor surrenders himself through a lust for power."[22]

All these considerations show that the priest who is ambitious for power and does not know how to make good use of his authority is really endangering himself and risking his eternal salvation: "By a frightening revenge of justice, whoever revels externally in a position of high authority digs a pit within himself for his own fall. He makes himself like an apostate angel, because, though he is a mere man, he disdains to be like men."[23]

Preserving the proper balance between humility and power is a difficult task. This achievement is the fruit of a very particular grace. Because of their natural inclinations ordinary men will be too likely to swerve to one side or the other. But in the following words from one of St. Leo's sermons for the anniversary of his election we find the balance perfectly expressed by one who evidently realizes both his own personal weakness and the magnitude of the dignity which has been laid upon him: "God's condescension, dearly beloved, has made this day a source of honor for me. By elevating my lowliness to this exalted position, He has shown that He spurns none of His children. Therefore, although I must tremble at the thought of my own unworthiness, still it is an act of piety to rejoice in God's gift. For He from whom this burden came will assist me in carrying it as I should. And lest my weak shoulders should collapse under the weight of God's gift, He will be my strength, who has bestowed on me this dignity.[24]

"Therefore, on the anniversary of the day on which it was the will of the Lord to invest me with the very source of the episcopal office, I have genuine reasons for rejoicing at this manifestation of God's glory in me; because, in order that He might be much loved by me, He forgave me much, and that He might show forth the wonders of His grace, He bestowed His gifts on one in whom He found no recommendation of merit."[25]

Only such filial sentiments of unlimited trust and confidence in God can offset in the priest the fear which naturally arises from realizing his own unfitness to wield the power of God. It is only by turning his eyes to heaven that he can keep from losing heart at what he sees in himself. Again St. Leo states this truth with his customary vigor and delicacy of expression: "As often as the mercy of God deigns to bring back the day of His great gifts to me, dearly beloved, I have good reasons for rejoicing if I refer my acceptance of this sublime office back to the praise of Him from whom it came. This act of reverence is suitable for all priests, but I realize that it is particularly necessary for myself, for with the importance of the office entrusted to me I must cry out in the words of the prophet: 'O Lord, I heard Thy word, and feared: I beheld Thy work, and trembled.'

"For what is so unusual or so alarming as work for a weak man, high position for an individual of low rank, and dignity for an undeserving person? Yet we do not despair nor do we lose heart, for we are not counting on ourselves, but rather on Him who works in us."[26]

In conclusion, to sum up briefly the viewpoint which should animate every priest in his use of his authority, we may cite the weighty words of St. Gregory the Great to the effect that the real joy of priests should not be so much to rule men as to help them.[27] They should never be so taken with the desire of appearing to be masters, as to forget that they are fathers. He reminds the priest of the dignity of his office and of the humility and lowliness which should mark its exercise, by referring back to the early origins of the priestly office in the Old Testament: "All who are in authority should pay less attention to the power of their position than to their own equality of nature with their subjects. Their joy should be not so much to rule men as to help them. They should bear in mind that our fathers of old were not kings of men, but shepherds of flocks."[28]

PART III

THE PRIEST AND HIMSELF

Chapter VIII

Devotion to Sacred Learning

THE priest's obligations of zeal, as has already
been pointed out, entail serious responsibilities
for the welfare of souls. In the discharge of these sacred
duties his greatest assistance comes from the sacramental grace of Holy Orders. The work of grace, however, does not supplant that of nature. Neither does
the influence of the divine character of Orders do away
with the natural gifts and attainments of the individual. The priest, like everyone else, must furnish
the natural foundation for the supernatural.

A very practical application of this heavy responsibility for others is found in the duty of self-prepara-
tion. To assume care of the eternal welfare of a spiritual family calls for the most perfect preparation possible, because of the tremendous eternal issues involved.
St. John Chrysostom utilizes the athletic background
of Greece to stress this important point: "When men
start out on an athletic career they need instructors

and trainers, special food and frequent exercise. A thousand and one precautions are called for, because weakness in only one detail can paralyze all their efforts and ruin their hopes.

"Now the mystical body of Christ is not at battle with material forces but with invisible powers. How will its guardians preserve it in all its vigor and perfection if they themselves are not men of superhuman virtue, who are thoroughly versed in the art of healing souls?"[1]

A very important element of this careful preparation for the priestly life consists in the acquisition of that intellectual background which will enable the priest to defend his faith and demonstrate to an unbelieving world that his acceptance of divine revelation is really a rational and justifiable submission of his intellect. No one will attempt a real "proof" of the dogmas of our faith. Still every priest must be sufficiently acquainted with the general background of dogmatic theology to be able to present Catholic belief intelligently and to show the reasonableness of the stand of the Church. Practical business ability in the priest, even though highly developed, cannot compensate for lack of familiarity with the substance and the proofs of the dogmatic teachings of the Church. Strange as it might seem, St. John Chrysostom affirms in no uncertain terms that not even holiness of life can replace knowledge of dogma:

"It is important that priests should be learned. If they are not, the Church suffers greatly. This explains why, along with other qualities, such as zeal for well-doing, meekness, and a blameless life, the Apostle mentions learning when he uses the word: Teacher.

"Why does he call the priest a teacher? Doubtless, you will say, in order that he may teach wisdom by good example. Everything else, you would say, is unessential because the priest does not need book-learning in order to lead his followers on the road to salvation. If that is so, then why does Paul mention clearly: 'Especially those who devote themselves to preaching and teaching.' How can mere holiness of life help us to explain dogmas?

"I am not referring to the kind of learning which makes a man vain and boastful or which is clothed in artificial elegance. I am speaking of the learning which is fed on strength of mind, which is full of prudence and common sense. Such learning is not based on mere rhetoric and eloquence, but on ideas; its foundation is not in happy phrasing but in truth."[2]

St. Gregory the Great points out this obligation in no less certain terms: "No one is so bold as to teach an art unless he has first mastered it by careful reflection. How rash it is, then, for the unskilled to take up the pastoral office, when the government of souls is the art of all arts. Everyone knows that the wounds of the soul are more difficult to heal than the wounds of the body. Yet oftentimes those who know nothing at all about spiritual things set themselves up as physicians of souls, while those who are unacquainted with pharmacy would blush to be called doctors."[3]

This same saint shows that the priest who is not learned in this good sense is failing in his duties toward others. Instead of enlightening and leading them on to higher things he blinds them and makes them stagger and fall under the burden of their sins: "The back is bent under dimming eyes (cf. Psalm 88:24) because when the leaders of the people lose the light of knowledge, the faithful who follow them are bent low in carrying the burden of their sins."[4]

The Fathers see in the pursuit of sacred learning the priest's most powerful natural contribution to preparing the way for divine grace in his own life and the life of others. Besides they find in devotion to the sacred sciences his surest safeguard against worldly contacts and influences. Hence it is, as St. Gregory observes, that sustained attention to the study of the sacred sciences assures the priest of faithful devotion to his sacred duties: "The priest lives up to all these sacred responsibilities if he is filled with the spirit of heavenly fear and love, and daily meditates on the commands of Holy Writ. This he does in order that the words of divine warning may re-enkindle the fervor of his watchfulness over his people and of his farsighted attention to the life of heaven within him. In all this he is motivated by the realization that whereas his contacts with the world are continually leading him away from his first fervor, he may by the spirit of compunction acquire new love for his spiritual home in heaven."[5]

This same lesson is emphasized by the special place which the priest occupies in the eyes of his people. Priests are, to use the expression of St. Ambrose, "interpreters of the faith." Every interpreter, to be worthy of the name, must have a thorough grasp of both the languages with which he works. He must understand questions in one language, translate them into another, and then receive in return and transmit the answers back into the language from which the questions originated. Without this ability no one can lay claim to the title of interpreter.

Now, the office of the priest is to find the answers to the questions of human life in the language of God. His next step is to express the language of God in terms that will be grasped by the people. In a word, he is an interpreter between God and man. Consequently, to be well-versed in the language of God he must be deeply devoted to the study of sacred science. Only in this study can he familiarize himself with the ideas and terms which will translate for the people God's answers to the questions of life. With these thoughts as his inspiration, St. Jerome insists so emphatically on knowledge of God's law as a requisite for the priesthood, that he concludes to the impossibility of having one without the other: "At the same time bear in mind that it is part of the priestly office to have an answer for whoever inquires about the law of God. If a man is a priest, he should know the law of the Lord. If he does not know the law, then by that very fact he proves that he is not a real priest."[6]

Hence the primary aim of the priest's acquisition of knowledge is to satisfy his obligation of equipping himself to help others. We have already remarked on the necessity of divine grace as the foundation of all zeal. Still it is familiarity with all the different aspects of the sacred sciences which normally serves as the indispensable prelude to the operations of grace. In this twofold strength, says St. Jerome, the priest is enabled to fulfill the prophecy of Malachias, to the effect that "the lips of the priest shall keep wisdom, and they shall seek the law at his mouth."[7] "Hence we may conclude from these words of Malachias, that the priest should be outstanding for his knowledge of the Law and the teaching of God, and that with the added assistance of spiritual grace, he may be so trained as to be able to confute his opponents." (Tit. 1, 9.)[8]

The absolute necessity of well-trained and fervent priests is brought into bolder relief when integrity of doctrine has been jeopardized by heresy. It was the sad experience of St. Leo the Great in his combats with the Monophysites to find himself at times battling almost single-handed not only against heretics and heresiarchs, but even against some unwary priests whom neglect of study had trapped in error. It was with these facts in mind that he wrote to the clergy and faithful of Constantinople to voice his complaints over the intellectual weakness of too many priests: "For if ignorance seems hardly tolerable in lay people, with still greater reason it can be neither excused nor pardoned in those who occupy positions of authority."[9]

Still, learning in the priest cannot be of the shallow and superficial kind which he encounters in so many of his contacts with the world. Because his office puts him under the obligation to do battle against the fatal consequences of such counterfeit learning, he must necessarily be equipped with more genuine and substantial knowledge. The authority of his sacred office is exposed to ridicule and contempt if it is not reinforced with a sure and thorough grasp of the principles which he champions. St. John Chrysostom describes the situation very clearly when he writes:

"You will find in the Church some individuals who are driven by rash curiosity to a kind of study which can do them no good and which cannot possibly succeed because it encounters incomprehensible mysteries. Others there are who demand of God explanations for His judgments and who wear themselves out in fruitless efforts to sound this unfathomable abyss. . . .

"You will find few persons who give themselves up seriously to the twofold pursuit of faith and virtue. A great many, we are told, go looking for what they will never find, even at the risk of arousing God's anger. For whenever we attempt to find out what He does not want us to know, not only is our energy wasted, since it cannot prevail against the will of God, but we run the risk of losing ourselves in our searchings — and, after all, this last would be the least of the ills which could befall us.

"Now if in the presence of such a disorder a priest tries simply to use his authority in order to silence these indiscreet searchers after wisdom, he will acquire a reputation for arrogance and incompetence. Hence he must be provided with solid learning if he is to escape such grave accusations and rescue men from the path of ruin.

"The priest's only help, the only weapon he can wield against the ideas and tendencies just mentioned, is the spoken word. If he does not know how to speak forcefully, then the souls entrusted to him are tossed about on the waves of error like little skiffs in a raging storm. . . . Consequently the priest should neglect nothing which can teach him the art of forceful preaching."[10]

Because of its close connection with the duties and functions of the priesthood, the possession of solid learning became very early in the history of the Church one of the distinctive marks of the sacerdotal calling. It was only at a comparatively late period that priests began to be distinguished from the laity and from the lower clergy by a special manner of dress. From the beginning their knowledge of God's law and of the things pertaining to faith was their chief claim to distinction, as Pope St. Celestine I pointed out in his fourth letter to the Bishops of the Province of Vienne: "We priests are to be distinguished from the people and from the rest of the clergy by our learning, not by our clothes; by our conduct rather than by our dress; and by purity of mind instead of by outward show."[11]

Besides the reasons just advanced by the Fathers for the necessity of thorough theological knowledge by all priests, there are others based on the evil effects which follow inevitably when a priest attempts to teach doctrine or to refute error without being solidly grounded in his fundamental principles. In such circumstances he will very naturally be inwardly conscious of his limitations. Then, because he realizes that the prestige and authority of his position are at stake, he will attempt to put on a false front by resorting to specious arguments, empty phrases, and blustering refutations. In all this he will be unaware that his manner only accentuates his ignorance. St. Jerome has portrayed this type of priest very realistically: "Nothing is more disgusting than the arrogance of uncouth priests who regard a glib tongue as a sign of learning and authority. They are always ready for an argument, and they thunder at the flock entrusted to them with high-sounding phrases."[12]

The somberness of this picture well explains the wish which the saint expresses for Nepotian in another letter: "I would not have you be a demagogue nor a rambling, wrangling talker. Rather I would like to see you well versed in the mysteries and intimately acquainted with the secrets of your God. To have only a facile tongue with an easy flow of words is a sign of ignorance."[13]

A certain amount of the theological knowledge which the Fathers regard as so indispensable for the sacerdotal ministry is acquired in the studies preceding ordination. It is not the mind of the Church, however, that the completion of these studies should terminate the mental training of her ministers. The seminary course accomplishes little more than provide an introduction to studies which should last a lifetime. Although St. Jerome's exhortation in the following passage is directed mainly to those who in his time were ordained without previous seminary training, still his words have a practical lesson for all priests when he exhorts them to "take care that, at least after their ordination to the priesthood, they should learn the law of God, in order that they may teach what they have themselves learned and in this way increase their learning rather than their wealth."[14]

In conclusion, St. Gregory the Great sees in priests who are well versed in sacred theology a most efficacious means of carrying on the apostolate of the Church to those outside her ranks. This point cannot be emphasized too strongly, particularly in modern times when the ever-increasing number of educated persons creates new problems of intellectual approach for the priest who desires to manifest the treasures of divine revelation to non-Catholics. With his customary taste for allegory the saint writes: "We must seek out well-formed and untiring teachers, who are in constant close contact with the teaching of the sacred volumes. They make known the unity of the Church and are like the bars put through the rings to carry the Ark. Carrying the Ark on bars is a symbol of the Church being brought by the preaching of good teachers to the untrained minds of those outside the fold (cf. Exodus 25)."[15]

St. Jerome describes the fruits of the priest's study when he writes in praise of his beloved Nepotian that "by sustained study and long meditation he had made of his heart a library of Christ."[16]

Chapter IX

The Priest and Worldliness

CLOSE relationship with Christ and a divinely constituted position of authority for the eternal welfare of the faithful demand that the whole background of priestly life should radiate spirituality. The priest must be "different" from other men in the world. As a man of God he is to exemplify his spiritual convictions by breaking with whatever characterizes a "man of the world." This does not mean being unnatural or insensible in ideal and outlook. Quite the contrary. With much more truth than the pagan poet, the priest should be able to say: *"Nihil humanum mihi alienum."* Nevertheless he cannot safely lose sight of the fact that he is not of the world, even though his life keeps him constantly in the world.

This obligation of diffusing spirituality reduces itself in large part to the negative duty of not being worldly. This obligation, in turn, implies something positive. It cannot be limited to the mere avoidance of sin. Certain attitudes which might be tolerated in persons of the world cannot be legitimately fostered in the conduct of the priest. The laity will find it difficult to respect a man who is officially a minister of the altar but whose interests and ideals go no higher than those of persons around him. Unless he rises above this common level, the priest will never succeed in lifting his flock to an appreciation of the higher interests of the Christian life.

St. Bernard stresses this point most vigorously: "Among people of the world trifles are trifles; in the mouth of the priest they are blasphemies. . . . Thou hast consecrated thy mouth to the Gospel: to open it to such things is unlawful, and to accustom it to them is sacrilege. 'The lips of the priest,' it is said, 'shall keep knowledge, and they shall seek the law at his mouth' — the law, not trifles or gossip.

"It is not enough to guard one's mouth against the light word which is passed off as a jest or a sign of good fellowship. The ear should not even be opened to such rude things. It is disgraceful to take part in mere chatter, and more disgraceful still to start it."[1]

The saint then presents the objection which is most frequently raised against this ideal. Although his remarks are directed against the abuse which then prevailed of clerics affecting military dress, the lesson which he inculcates has its application to other aspects of ecclesiastical life as well: "They usually answer: 'Is not God more concerned with what we do than with what we wear?' Yes, but this type of dress indicates a distorted mentality and unbecoming conduct. Why do clerics want to be one thing while appearing to be another, especially when what they want to appear has less of the spirit of chastity and sincerity? Trying to dress like soldiers and to act like clerics, they are really

neither in their conduct. They do not fight like soldiers, nor do they preach the Gospel like clerics. To
what class do they really belong? *Trying to belong to
both, they end up by belonging to neither.*"[2]

In a letter which was intended to put his spiritual
daughter, St. Eustochium, on her guard, St. Jerome
draws on his choicest gifts of biting sarcasm to portray
the ridiculous behavior of the clerical "playboy" who
is so thoroughly taken up with worldly ways and gossip
that the saint calls him contemptuously the "city's
messenger-boy:"

"I really am ashamed to continue, lest I appear to
be nursing a grudge rather than giving an admonition.
There are some individuals — I speak of men belonging to my own order — who would seem to have de-
sired the priesthood or the diaconate for no other
purpose than to make more of an impression on wom-
en. Their whole interest is centered in their clothes.
They are careful to be well perfumed and they take
care that the skin of their feet is smooth and does not
wrinkle. Their hair has been waved with a curling-
iron. Their fingers sparkle with rings, and lest the
damp street should wet the soles of their feet they
hardly dare to walk even on tip-toes. At the sight of
such persons you would take them for newlyweds instead of clerics. Some of them have made it their life's
specialty to become acquainted with the names, resi-
dences, and habits of the city's dowagers.

"I shall describe briefly one of these men, who is a
past master of this art, so that from your knowledge
of the master you may the more easily recognize his

followers. He is up bright and early at sunrise. This importunate old man arranges the order of his visits, looks up his street-maps, and rushes into the bedrooms of his friends almost before they are awake. If he espies a nice cushion, an elegant mantle, or some piece of household furniture, he praises it, admires it, and fondles it, and while complaining that he has not such fine things for himself, he does not ask for them as much as he extorts them, because all of these ladies are fearful of offending the city's messenger-boy.

"This man is no friend of chastity; he is an enemy of fasting. He can tell foods by their aromas, and delights in choice meats. His language is rough and uncouth and always ready for abuse. Wherever you turn, he is the first person you meet. He always is starting or spreading the latest rumor. His horses are changed for him at set times, and they are so sleek and lively that to see him you would think that he were the brother of the king of Thrace."[3]

It would be a serious mistake to conclude from passages of this kind that the Fathers wished to enjoin on the clergy so complete a separation from the world that they were never to come into anything but professional and ecclesiastical contact with the laity. Social intercourse is a necessary element of the priestly ministry in order to acquire, preserve, and develop the good will which is necessary for the efficient and fruitful exercise of the apostolate. But even here there must be discretion and proper balance. Consequently, the priest must show a discerning spirit in recognizing when his presence is necessary or useful in purely social circles. He should not display an indiscriminate interest in social gatherings, but should be able to see when it is more expedient to decline than to accept the many invitations which will surely come to him. St. Jerome stresses the love that priests should have for all homes, and their obligation of not being unceasingly in contact with the social world: "With much greater reason than physicians ought we, to whom the healing of souls has been entrusted, to love the homes of all Christians as our own! Nevertheless let them receive us rather as comforters in their sorrows than as dinner-guests in their prosperity. People soon lose respect for the cleric who is often invited out to dinner and who does not sometimes decline."[4]

In this same letter to Nepotian, St. Jerome answers the objection which would justify excessive and unnecessary worldly contacts on the grounds of their supposed necessity for the welfare of souls: "You should avoid the lavish banquets of worldlings, particularly when there is question of those in high position. It is a disgrace for the lictors of the consuls and for bands of soldiers to be waiting outside the doors of a priest of Christ, who was poor and crucified and who begged His bread from others. It is not right for the judge of the province to find better meals in your house than in his own palace.

"But should you object that you do these things in order to gain his good-will in favor of those who are poor and in misery, I answer that the judge will have more respect for a quiet-loving and retired cleric than for a rich one, and will be much more impressed by your sanctity than by your wealth."[5]

Perhaps few of the Fathers have insisted more vigorously than St. John Chrysostom on the unworldly atmosphere which should mark the life of the priest. Hence it is interesting to see at the same time how he requires the priest to be well acquainted with persons and things of the world, because of the fact that he is ordained for men: "Priests are the salt of the earth. . . . It is not enough to be pure in order to accept these sublime functions; prudence and a wide range of knowledge are just as necessary. The priest must be well versed even in worldly affairs, and in these matters he should be as much at home as persons whose whole interest is absorbed by them.

"At the same time he must remain as foreign to these things as the hermits who spend their lives on mountain-tops. In his contact with married persons who have children to raise, servants to direct, large estates to manage, perhaps even government affairs to handle, or state business to transact, the priest must be able to adapt himself to all these varied situations.

"I do not mean by this that he is expected to be two-faced, a flatterer, or a hypocrite. What I mean is simply this, that he should comport himself in all these situations with full confidence and perfect freedom of action, that he should in all prudence adapt himself to varying circumstances, and be at one and the same time filled with mildness and seriousness.

"In fact, it is impossible to handle all men in the same way. Doctors do not prescribe the same medicines for all diseases. No pilot uses the same kind of maneuvering against all kinds of wind. The vessel which the priest guides is likewise tossed about by constant storms. Nor do all these storms come from the outside; at times their roar is heard in the very heart of the ship. In these circumstances how much moderation and energy are called for! Now all these things, different though they are in themselves, tend toward one sole end which is the glory of God and the welfare of the Church."[6]

The saint continues to point out that just as the natural weakness of the priest makes him tend to exaggeration in the use of his authority, so this same natural frailty will tend to upset the proper balance in his necessary relationships with the interests of persons in the world:

"Because of the excessive interest shown by priests in worldly affairs we have the disagreements, misunderstandings, and scandals which we encounter almost daily. Priests are given titles which are more in keeping with worldly establishments, when, as a matter of fact, their titles should come only from their sacred functions. The names they are given should come from care for the poor, help for the unfortunate, the spirit of hospitality, interest in the oppressed, care for orphans, the defense of widows, and the protection of virgins. Priests should be engaged in these activities rather than in the care of fields and houses. Those activities of charity are the real treasures of the Church; they are the kind of wealth which brings joy to our hearts and is advantageous for you at the same time that it brings you genuine satisfaction. . . .

"In our day God's priests devote their time to wine-making, harvesting and the sale and purchase of fruit. Under the Old Law priests were excused from this kind of work, even though their functions did call for a certain acquaintance with worldly matters. Yet we who are admitted into the secrets of heaven, we who enter into the Holy of Holies, we, I say, take the place of merchants and inn-keepers. That is why we neglect Sacred Scripture, why our prayers are listless, and why we disregard our other duties. It is impossible to divide one's interests and to devote equal care and attention to these two fields of activity."[7]

The foolishness of thus attempting to conciliate two ways of life and to get the best out of two contrary worlds, is emphasized in the inevitable difficulties of all such efforts.

"If a bishop does not spend his time going from house to house every day and paying more visits than lawyers, people will be offended beyond all expression. Not only the sick but also those who are well will want his visits, not out of a spirit of religion or a sense of piety but in order to be singled out for marks of honor and deference. Should it happen that a bishop pays more visits to persons of wealth and power, acting thus for the interests of the Church or even under the force of necessity, he will be called a favor-seeker and a flatterer.

"But why should we be speaking merely of the visits of bishops? A mere word of theirs has often given rise to such serious accusations that we have seen some men waste away and even die of sorrow. People watch even the expression of their face. Their simplest gestures, the tone of their voice, the movements of their eyes — everything is watched, everything is weighed in the balance. 'He gave that man a very amiable smile,' they will say. 'He greeted that other quite pleasantly and meaningly, while he returned my greeting with cold reserve and as if out of a sense of duty.' "[8]

In a word, to borrow the expression of the Apostle, the priest is to use the world as though using it not. The inconsistency of a cleric whose mind is taken up with worldly interests is stressed by St. Gregory the Great in one of his homilies for the Ember Saturday in September. Taking his theme from the cure of the woman who was unable to look up, he sees in her an image of the soul whose interests are centered on earth. Then he recalls the passage of Leviticus[9] which disqualifies hunchbacks from the priesthood: "Moses commanded that no hunchbacks were to be admitted to the priesthood. All of us have been redeemed by the blood of Christ and have been made members of one same High Priest. . . . But because a hunchback is always looking down, he is barred from the priesthood. For whoever is intent only on the things of earth is witness against himself that he is not a member of our great High Priest."[10]

The priest should have no fear that he will be the loser by thus cutting himself off from the world; he actually will gain more than he gives up. He detaches himself generously from small satisfactions within the limited orbit of his own life, and in return becomes partaker in all the good and noble things of the entire world. By spiritualizing the old proverb of the pagans,

Omne forti solum patria, St. Ambrose pictures most attractively for the ministers of the sanctuary the influence of the unworldly spirit on priestly life: "Let there be no dread of exile for the wise man who recalls that the world is his fatherland, nor fear of want when it is remembered that for the wise man the whole world is filled with riches. What is more noble than the man who is immune to the attractions of gold, who has only contempt for wealth, and who looks down, as it were, from an impregnable fortress on the fleeting desires of men? Whoever has reached this point is rightly regarded by his fellow-men as a super-man."[11]

With his wonted bluntness St. Jerome points out eloquently why the clergy must be unworldly in their viewpoint and in their conduct, and at the same time expresses his contempt for the cleric who is unfaithful to this ideal of his vocation:

"The cleric who is in the service of the Church of Christ should first of all grasp the full meaning of his title. Then when he has defined his name, he should try to live up to it. For if *kleros* in Greek is the same as *sors* in Latin, these individuals are called clerics either because the Lord is their lot or portion, or because they belong to the lot of the Lord.

"But whoever is either the lot of the Lord or has the Lord for his portion ought to live in such a way that he may possess the Lord and be in turn possessed by the Lord. For my part, so long as I am in the service of the altar I live on what is offered at the altar. So long as I have food and clothing, with these I am satisfied, and thus naked will I follow the naked cross. . . .

"I beseech you, then, not to be searching for worldly gain in the army of Christ; do not begin to be richer than in the beginning of your clerical life. Let the poor and the traveler be frequent guests at your frugal table, and may Christ be in their midst as a fellow-guest. Should you come in contact with the trafficking cleric, or with one who has risen from poverty to riches, or to a high station from obscurity, avoid him as you would flee the plague."[12]

In conclusion, we may cite a moving passage from St. Bernard wherein he demonstrates how the unworldly cleric approaches as closely as possible to the perfect likeness of his Divine Master:

"He is a faithful pontiff who views with the eyes of a dove all the good things which pass through his hands, whether they be God's gifts to man or man's offerings to God, and still holds back nothing for himself. He looks out, not for the gifts of the people but rather for their advancement in virtue, and does not arrogate God's glory to himself.

"He does not wrap up his talent in a napkin but turns it over to the bankers, not for himself but for his Lord. He has no hole like the foxes, nor nests like the birds, nor a purse like Judas. Finally, with Mary he has no room in the inn. He imitates perfectly Him who had not where to lay His head, and in this world makes himself as a broken vase, to be doubtless later on a vessel unto honor, not unto shame. Finally he loses his life in this world, that he may keep it unto life everlasting."[13]

Chapter X

The Priest and Money

ALTHOUGH to be in the world while not of the world is the ideal for the priest, nevertheless, he cannot break off all contact with the interests of the men from whose ranks he was taken. Since money occupies so large a place in the lives of most men, the priest will have to adopt a definitely supernatural attitude toward things financial.

This is all the more true if his pastoral duties put him in contact with the financial administration of a parish. Here particularly he must distinguish between use and abuse, between necessity and superfluity. By virtue of the law of the Gospel and the example of the Apostles he is entitled by strict right to receive material support from his flock and to make collections for the relief of the poor and needy. St. Paul invoked this right when he appealed to the authority of the Gospel to vindicate himself against criticism for accepting support from the faithful of Corinth.

If the priest received from the faithful only his material maintenance and nothing beyond, there would be no danger of excessive interest in money. But the generosity of the flock surrounds the shepherd with many more good things than he actually needs. At the same time, as a steward, the priest must often handle more or less considerable sums in his apostolate of charity or in the material expansion of his work. St. Bede sensed this necessity and took advantage of it to warn against a rigoristic misinterpretation of our Lord's prohibition of laying aside money and carrying purses: "We should not think that these words strictly forbid the saints to lay aside any money at all, either for their own use or to relieve the necessities of the poor. We read that our Lord Himself, who was ministered to by angels, nevertheless, in order to instruct His Church, had a treasury, kept the offerings of the faithful, and used them for His own needs and for those of other poor persons. The meaning of these words is that we should not serve God because of these things, and that fear of want should not make us deviate from the practice of justice.."[1]

Consequently, there are few priests who have not some contact with money. Because of the weakness of human nature, every priest is likewise exposed to the danger of overstepping the bounds of necessity and allowing himself to be unduly influenced by the attractions of money and the comforts it can provide. He may not realize that, as St. Paul warned Timothy, the desire of money is the root of all evil.[2] This explains also why this same Apostle, who was so insistent on collections for the poor of Jerusalem[3] and who defended with such vigor his own right to support.[4] yet felt obliged to warn his beloved Timothy not to desire more than this, but to bear ever in mind that "godliness with contentment is indeed great gain,"[5] that the true priest and bishop will be content with food and sufficient clothing and that "those who seek to become rich fall into temptation and a snare and into many useless and harmful desires which plunge men into destruction and damnation."[6] From the tone of these warnings of the great Apostle we can see whence St. John Chrysostom drew the certainty with which he wrote centuries later: "Lust for money is old leaven; it will soil any place or house where it is found."[7]

St. Paul's correlation of the priest's right to support and his apostolic ministry provided the Fathers of succeeding ages with one of their chief inspirations in their portrayal of the priestly ideal. It is interesting to note that they make material support dependent, not on the mere fact of being a priest, but on the actual performance of priestly work and fidelity to priestly ideals. St. Paul had written: "If any man will not work, neither let him eat."[8] Any other mode of life would mean accepting support under false pretenses. St. John Chrysostom is still more explicit: "The Apostle is not satisfied merely with proving that the priest is worthy of his hire. He goes farther and sketches the portrait of the ideal priest of Christ. He needs the courage of the soldier, the patience of the farmer, and the watchfulness of the shepherd. When he has acquired these qualities, he is entitled to his support, but to no more."[9]

It would be wrong, however, to conclude that the priest's right to support from his ministry places him in a position of undue dependence on the faithful or in any way degrades his sacerdotal dignity. It would

be no less erroneous to think that the people are thereby entitled to exercise any kind of authority over the
priest whom it is their duty and privilege to support.
The faithful are as much in need of the spiritual serv-
ices of God's minister as he is of their material assistance. This correlation contributes to the interest and
welfare of both parties, without elevating the one or
debasing the other. This practical and all-important
thought furnishes St. John Chrysostom with the theme
of the following passages from one of his commentaries
on the epistles to the Corinthians:

"We must admire the prudence of St. Paul and note
the tact with which he makes his point. He does not
say: 'Those who exercise sacred functions live at the
expense of those who employ them,' but rather: 'they
live by these functions.' In this way he does not injure
the feelings of those who receive this support nor the
humility of those who provide it.

"That is why he does not say: 'Those who minister
at the altar receive gifts from those who present victims,' but that 'they have their share with the altar.'
In the same way he does not say that priests are entitled
to offerings, but that they 'live by their functions.'
Thus he wished to show that the priest should not be
a money-seeker nor try to become wealthy through the
ministry."[10]

The confident expectation of support from his flock,
with the realization that he should seek no further re-
muneration from the exercise of his sacred functions,
is the faithful priest's most potent safeguard against the
snares of avarice. At least in most cases, priests un-

doubtedly will be provided with much more than mere support and even with more than the ordinary comforts of life. But since the generosity of his people aims precisely to free him from all anxious concern over the material side of his life, it would be lamentable indeed were he to misuse this very generosity in order to make of himself a "moneyed man," or a man of comfort and ease. This is, of course, a very human possibility, but St. John Chrysostom would have every priest convinced of the essentially spiritual background of his sacerdotal life, and points out the evident parallelism between the ministers of the Gospel and the Levites of the Old Law:

"Priests should be generously provided with all the necessities of life, lest they suffer want or fall into discouragement and lest, while busying themselves with details, they neglect more important matters. An added reason is that they may develop an attachment for spiritual things and have no worries over temporal interests.

"Such were the Levites of the Old Law. They did not busy themselves with material interests, because the laity saw to all this for them. The Law assured them an income, such as tithes, money offerings, first fruits of the earth, offerings for the priests, and many other things. It was only proper that the Law should make these provisions for those who were occupied with spiritual things. Still I maintain that priests are entitled to nothing more than food or clothing, lest they become ensnared in worldly interests."[11]

When St. John Chrysostom declares with his customary bluntness that "priests are entitled to nothing more than food and clothing" he should not be interpreted so literally as to demand that Christ's ministers live in squalor and misery. Experience with human nature had brought him into contact with certain overzealous and ill-enlightened souls, who misinterpreted the priestly spirit of poverty as a synonym for niggardliness and mendicancy. To be poor in spirit the priest need not be a pauper, much less go begging his sustenance. The almost harsh rigor of St. John Chrysostom softens considerably in order to impress this point definitely on the minds of his hearers:

"After all, is it unseemly for the priest to live in comfort? Does comfort mean that he is clothed with silk, that he is always surrounded by a crowd of admirers, that he rides a richly caparisoned horse, or builds luxurious houses? If he does, then I will be the first to blame him, and I shall be merciless. I shall tell him quite plainly that such conduct is unworthy of the priesthood. How will he ever protect his brethren against such frivolity, if he does not first protect himself?

"But because it is unseemly for a priest to have more than is necessary, does it follow from this that he must go around like a beggar, with his hand out? You yourself, his disciple, would be ashamed of him. If your father according to the flesh acted thus. you would protest against the disgrace, but when it is question of your spiritual father, why do you not blush and slink away in the darkness? Is not the disgrace of the father the shame of his children?[12] Will you, then, have your priests die of hunger? Piety cannot allow that, nor can God approve it.

"I am aware that those who feel themselves reproached by these explanations usually ask, 'Is it not written: *Do not keep gold, or silver, or money in your girdles, or two tunics, or a staff?*'[13] Even while they ask this question, the words which they quote do not prevent them from having three or four sets of clothing and soft beds. . . . If I ask them how it happens that they do not apply this text to themselves, they make answer that only their masters are obliged to perfection. When St. Paul wrote: 'But having food and clothing with these let us be content'[14] was he speaking only to priests? No; assuredly not, but to all men. This is quite clear from a simple examination of the context. After saying: 'Godliness with contentment is indeed great gain,' he added: 'For we brought nothing into the world, and certainly we can take nothing out.' Then he concludes: 'But having food with sufficient clothing, with these let us be content. But those who seek to become rich fall into temptation and a snare and into many useless and harmful desires.' "[15]

Even of the priest who aims at being a model of poverty the Fathers expect a sense of economy and a certain acquaintance with financial problems. They look for that even balance which will safeguard the integrity of his sacerdotal ideal and provide for the interests of the Church, the poor, and the good works which the Church is rightly expected to inaugurate and foster. Neither can the priest neglect the Christlike duty of tenderness for the poor, or of hospitality for travelers. There are occasions, consequently, when even priests must take the initiative and go out in search of money. In such circumstances they are to be careful to exercise zeal for souls without offending the good will of those who are expected to assist them with their donations. In a word they must cultivate a practical sense of *savoir-faire* side by side with the other virtues of the priestly life:

"Still mildness and patience are not enough for him who is placed in charge of a church. He must, in addition, have a sense of economy, for without this quality he will waste what belongs to the poor. . . . Foresight in this regard must be balanced by good judgment in order that church goods may be neither plentiful nor too few.

"The poor should be given promptly what is intended for them by the generosity of the faithful, and the Church should receive the balance, in keeping with the pious intentions of the donors. We should not forget to lay aside funds for entertaining guests or caring for the sick.

"Prudence and economy are no less necessary when there is question of soliciting or accepting donations. We must know how to persuade the wealthy to give donations with eagerness and joy. As we go about providing for the needs of the poor, we must take care not to hurt the feelings of benefactors."[16]

Still, even with the very best of good will, and notwithstanding earnest efforts at detachment, the priest will inevitably find himself surrounded with the

choicer things of life. Very often he will be provided
with far more than is requisite merely for his ordinary
support. No one can hope to avoid this danger when
even the austere and gruff St. Jerome had to complain
of the inroads which delicacies had supposedly made
into his rigid life. He paints a graphic picture: "Born
though I was in a poor house and in a country hut, I
who was scarcely able to quiet my growling stomach
with millet and coarse bread, am now hardly satisfied
with sweetbread. I know the names and the different
kinds of fish, and am an expert in telling where fowl
has come from. I find delight in the rarity of precious
foods."[17]

It is an interesting study in human nature to see
the rugged and emaciated Jerome thus berating himself for his self-styled sensuality. Yet in his devotion
to the cause of priestly holiness he may be pardoned
any seeming exaggeration. He warns against a danger
which confronts priests at the present time no less
than in Jerome's day. It is chiefly this which claims our
attention here. At the same time he points out how
considerate love of the poor is one of the most powerful safeguards which can be thrown up around God's
representatives when he writes: "It is the glory of a
bishop to provide for the wants of the poor. It is a
disgrace for any priest to be intent on increasing his
own wealth."[18]

Hence it is in generous almsgiving that the priest
will find the perfect outlet for the superfluous goods
which may happen to be his lot in the exercise of his
sacred ministry. If he is faithful to his calling, it is

into the hands of God's poor that his excess riches must ultimately find their way.

In the question of almsgiving the priest must, however, avoid the two extremes of parsimony and extravagance. In this connection the following advice of St. Ambrose is so practical and so applicable to present-day circumstances that it could have been set down by a twentieth-century rather than by a fifth-century bishop:

"It is evident that there must be some norm for liberality, lest useless alms be given. Moderation in almsgiving must be observed, especially by priests, lest their charity be more for show than an act of justice. No one is bothered more than the priest by requests for help. To him come the well and strong, and those who have no other reason for coming than that they have nothing else to do. Those persons want to use up what is reserved for the poor, and thus they empty the treasury. Still more, not satisfied with smaller offerings, they ask for larger alms, bolstering up their demands with the false garb of the poor and making themselves look like the sons of beggars.

"If the priest believes all these people readily, he will soon exhaust what he has laid aside to feed the poor. So there must be method in our alms-giving, lest the worthy go away empty-handed and the life-funds of the poor thus become the spoils of frauds. Let this, then, be the measure of your charity: that kindness be not forgotten, nor poverty be left unaided."[19]

St. Jerome warns that in all almsgiving the priest must be on his guard lest his seeming love for the poor degenerate into an indirect means of self-aggrandizement. It is not at all impossible for a priest to be activated by genuine love of the poor and with this laudable incentive to begin collecting means to alleviate their want. If he forgets that money, even when collected for holy purposes, has a natural fascination, he may easily fall victim to the temptation to appropriate these riches of the poor for his own advantage. In no uncertain terms St. Jerome stigmatizes the priest who has been thus victimized by the charms of "filthy lucre": "There are some who make small contributions to the poor, in order that they in turn may receive greater donations, and under the pretext of almsgiving they seek to amass riches. Such conduct should be termed hunting rather than almsgiving. That is the way we catch fish, birds, and wild beasts — putting a little bait on a hook, in order to catch the purses of society ladies."[20]

In concluding these reflections on the proper attitude of the priest toward money, we may quote a wise and prudent passage from St. Ambrose. In his treatise on the duties of ministers of the altar, the great bishop of Milan explains to his readers that there is danger of two extremes in the priestly viewpoint on things financial: too much attention, and too little attention. Then he declares that the true sacerdotal ideal follows the line of the golden mean: "Hence let your works of piety train you to justice, continence, and meekness. Being strengthened and well-grounded in faith, avoid the foolishness of youth and fight the good fight of faith. Do not involve yourself in worldly business for you are in the service of God. . . .

"You will have peace of mind and will be discreet in your use of worldly goods when your heart is neither set on the acquisition of riches, nor troubled by the fear of want."[21]

Lastly we find in a sermon which is attributed to St. Augustine an eloquent summary of the effects of the spirit of detachment in drawing the priest ever closer to Christ:

"We are the ministers and the servants of God. True servants of God are not those who serve to the eye only but who are faithful in obeying the will of the Lord in all things. These servants attain to such intimacy with their Master that they are no longer called servants but friends.

"Consequently, with our whole heart let us show our loyalty in much tribulation, in knowledge, in charity unfeigned, in watchings, in prisons and stripes, in the word of truth. And thus, while owning nothing we shall possess all things. This is the life of the blessed; this is the salvation of priests."[22]

Chapter XI

The Spirit of Chastity

FEW priestly qualities receive more enthusiastic praise from the Fathers than the holy virtue of chastity. Then, as now, the common opinion of the faithful, and even of those outside the fold, saw in this virtue the outstanding ornament of the priestly character. Many of the other sacerdotal virtues of the priest are shared by those in other walks of life. The virtues of the priest are oftentimes the same as the virtues of the faithful, though they exist in him in a more eminent degree. But in his vocation to celibacy, which he shares with those who profess the religious life, the priest stands unique among men. Writing on the dignity and duties of the episcopal state, St. Bernard brings into bold relief this distinctly privileged character of priestly continence:

"Nothing is more comely than chastity. It purifies what was conceived of sin-stained seed, makes a friend of an enemy, and an angel out of a man. There is, indeed, a difference between an angel and a chaste man, but this difference is one of actual bliss, not of the degree of virtue.

"Although the chastity of the angel is admittedly

more blissful, the chastity of a man shows far more strength. In the circumstances of this mortal life, it is chastity alone which foreshadows the state of unending glory. In the midst of those who marry, chastity alone evidences the life of that blessed region in which they neither marry nor are given in marriage, while it affords some foretaste of that same heavenly mode of life."[1]

Then he makes a more particular application of the beauty of chastity in the priesthood: "Consequently, I would say that this quality of such great beauty is a worthy adornment for the priesthood. It makes the priest beloved of God and of men, for his memory is not passed on in carnal succession but in the blessings of the spirit. And although his lot is still cast in this region which is so unlike heaven, yet chastity gives him a likeness with the glory of the saints."[2]

Much of this same thought had already been voiced by St. Augustine. On this point the Bishop of Hippo observes: "Remember that you are called to lead the life of angels upon earth. The angels neither marry nor are they given in marriage. This is what we shall be after the resurrection.[3] How great, then, is your dignity, you who begin to be even upon this earth what most men will be only after the resurrection!"[4]

The need of chastity is a natural outgrowth of the priest's separation from the world and of his nearness to God. He must be pure and holy if he is to enter worthily into the presence of God, and be a worthy mediator of grace for sinful men. This, as St. Ambrose points out, was sensed even under the Old Law:

"The people were chastened over a period of from two to three days, so that they might approach the altar of sacrifice in purity. That is why we read in the Old Testament: 'And they washed their garments.'

"Now if such care was taken in what was only a symbol of reality, what shall we say now of the reality itself? O priest and deacon, learn what it means to wash your garments, in order that you may bring a pure and unspotted body to the celebration of the holy mysteries. If the simple people were forbidden to draw near with their victim unless they had first washed their garments, will you, unwashed in mind and in body, presume to intercede for others and to be their minister?"[5]

If chastity is such a priceless ornament in the priestly character, even natural prudence requires that it be surrounded with every safeguard. High ideals and holy ambitions are no sure bulwark in themselves against the deceptive weakness of human nature. This being the case, the priest of God must, first of all, be adamant in refraining from liberties which are forbidden to the simple layman. He must then go farther and still be equally resolute even against those occasions which might be harmless for the laity, but which can hardly be reconciled with the ideals and aims of one who has consecrated himself entirely to divine things. St. Augustine stressed this point in a sermon to those who are vowed to chastity: "But you who have vowed yourselves to God should take care to keep closer watch over your body. You should not slacken the reins of concupiscence even in the face of what is permitted. In this way you will not only be on your guard against serious falls, but you will even turn aside from looks which are not in themselves sinful."[6]

From this it follows that it is particularly impossible in the matter of chastity to apply the same standard of judgment to the conduct of the priest and that of the layman. It is true that sin is sin, no matter by whom it is committed. Nevertheless some details of conduct or mentality which might pass unnoticed in the laity assume much graver importance in the life of a man who is a minister of God and a model for others. The only difference between the law of God for him and for them is that this law is more exacting for the shepherd than for the sheep. Hence St. Leo wrote in one of his letters: "The office of the priesthood is on such a high plane that things which are not regarded as faults for other members of the Church must nevertheless be looked upon as unlawful for priests."[7]

Thus the priest's precautions must be kept always on the same higher plane on which his continence is enshrined. It would be difficult to find a more direct or more practical synthesis of these precautions than in the following extract from St. Jerome's letter to Nepotian:

"Let the feet of women never, or at least but rarely, cross the threshold of your humble home. In your dealings with young girls and the virgins of Christ, have no favorites. Either love them all equally, or ignore them all equally. Dwell not under the same roof with them, and put no trust in the chastity of your past life. You cannot expect to be holier than David, nor wiser than Solomon. Remember always that a woman was responsible for the first dweller in Paradise being expelled from his home.

"In sickness prefer to be assisted by one of your holy brethren, by your mother or some other relative, or by a woman of unspotted integrity and stainless reputation. If you cannot find nurses among your relatives or among persons of unquestionable chastity, the Church has many matrons who can perform this service for you and thus gain some profit for themselves, so that you can by your sickness bring them the benefit of an alms. I know of some men who have regained the health of the body only to lose thereby the health of their soul. There is danger in the attentions of one on whose face you frequently look.

"If your priestly duties oblige you to visit a widow or a virgin, never go into her house alone. Have with you companions whose company cannot do harm to your reputation. If you are accompanied by a Lector, an Acolyte, or a Cantor, their adornment should not be in their apparel but rather in their conduct. They should not be putting waves into their hair but should let their external comportment be an assurance of modest reserve.

"Never be alone with a woman, off by yourselves, without witness or judge. If she has some personal matters to discuss, she can go to her matron at home or to some virgin or to some widow or married woman. She is surely not so unlike everyone else as to have no one but you in whom she can confide.

"Beware of whatever can arouse suspicion. Take care to avoid beforehand anything which might possibly give rise to gossip. Holy love has nothing to do with frequent presents of handkerchiefs, hair-ribbons, face-veils and special foods, or with flattering and sentimental letters.

"On the stage we blush at the amusements and the witticisms, the pleasantries and the other nonsense of lovers; we detest this kind of thing even in dignified men of the world. With how much greater reason, then, are we ashamed of these things in monks and clerics, for the priesthood of the latter is adorned by their profession of chastity, and the profession of chastity by the former receives new splendor from their priesthood.

"I do not mention these things because I fear for you or for other holy men, but because in every walk of life, in every rank and sex we find both good and bad and the condemnation of the bad is the praise of the good."[8]

These warnings are inescapably necessary when we consider the many dangers of chastity which lie hidden in the priest's unavoidable social contacts for the zealous discharge of his ministry. St. Augustine had already remarked, even to his simple faithful, that we have not put on Christ so thoroughly as to have kept nothing of the old Adam. Mindful of this fundamental and persistent weakness of human nature, St. John Chrysostom mentions in detail how the priest's chastity is endangered even in his necessary associations with women, and shows how this peril is ever present because of the constant duty of allowing women as well as men to profit by the benefits of his pastoral ministry:

"Because he is responsible for his entire flock, the spiritual director cannot give all his attention to men and neglect the women. They call for even special attention, by reason of their very weakness. To keep them from harm there is need of greater care than for men, or at the very least of equal care.

"They must be visited in times of sickness, consoled in their sorrows and assisted in their work. It is precisely in favor of these works of zeal that the Evil One will find a thousand ways to make the priest slip up, unless he is constantly on his guard. It is not only the eye of the woman of ill-fame but also that of the virtuous woman which can strike down and wreck a soul: her flattery softens the heart; her praise and her marks of respect make it a slave. Thus even the most ardent charity, which is the source of all good, becomes for the imprudent priest the source of all evil."[9]

Another point which St. John Chrysostom stresses vigorously is that the chastity of the priest is exposed to far greater dangers than that of the monk or the religious:

"Once more, we are not discussing how to command an army, nor how to rule an army or to rule a state, but rather how to fulfil functions which would call for the virtue of an angel. The soul of the priest should be purer than the rays of the sun; the Holy Ghost should be always with him and he should be able to say at all times: 'I live, now not I, but Christ lives in me.'[10]

"Those who live in the desert, far from the noise of the city and the bustle of the marketplace, are, so to speak, in a quiet harbor where the sky is always clear. Yet even they do not count too much on the protection which this kind of life affords them. They take a thousand precautions and leave nothing undone in their words or in their actions, to make of their heart an inviolable sanctuary and to preserve intact that purity which allows them to commune with God, insofar as human strength is capable of doing so.

"If such be the case for monks, then what vigilance and energy should not the priest exert in order to preserve his soul from every stain and to keep his spiritual beauty from every blemish. His state of life calls for greater purity than that of solitaries. His very calling as a priest lays him open to greater dangers. He can guard against these dangers only by unwearying watchfulness over himself. The beauty of a face, affected daintiness of movements and attitudes, listless talking, the lying colors of tinted eyelashes and painted cheeks, the artful arrangement and brilliance of dyed hair, richness of apparel, the attraction of gold and precious stones — in a word, everything which serves for the adornment of women, all this can disturb the mind of the priest, unless he is constantly protected by the arms of prudence and modesty."[11]

It is in view of the prime importance of sacerdotal chastity that St. John Chrysostom, in his second homily on St. Paul's Epistle to Titus, pointed out that the great Apostle does not require of priests mere purity of life, but a blameless reputation and conduct which

will exclude even the suspicion of evil.[12] In connection
with this passage, one cannot but recall St. Jerome's insistence that the sincere priest will protect his chastity
by avoiding ahead of time anything at all that might
possibly give rise to suspicion.

The natural consequence of the preceding considerations is that the entire atmosphere of a priest's
life must be redolent of the spiritual world into which
the profession of chastity naturally leads him. His outward conduct needs to be marked by the reserve and
decorum so naturally expected of one who is devoted,
body and soul, to higher things. Speaking only of the
laity, Tertullian observed that "it is not enough for
Christian modesty to exist, but it also should be seen."
Then he proceeds to show how interior ideals normally
tend to manifest themselves in external conduct:
"Christian modesty should be so perfect as to overflow
from the soul on to one's external comportment and
to well up from the depths of conscience to the plane
of outward life. It wishes to find in external behavior
an adornment worthy of the sacred obligation which
is to be kept inviolate forever."[13]

This beautiful ideal cannot be fully and fruitfully
realized if the obligations entailed by priestly celibacy
are regarded in the purely negative light of privations
and sacrifices. The inspiration for withstanding the
many difficulties of a life of chastity must be drawn
from the positive realization of its benefits and its
advantages in the life of the priest. It was with this idea
in mind that Tertullian, writing to his wife, called attention to the thoughts which are the Christian's in-

centive to a generous practice of chastity: "Continence was pointed out to us Christians by the Lord as a means of salvation, as a means of gaining eternal life, as a testimony of our faith, and as a preparation of this flesh of ours for the coming garment of incorruptibility."[14]

We may well conclude these thoughts on the value and beauty of priestly chastity with the profound question which St. Columbanus asks in chapter 6 of his *Regula Coenobialis,* where he stresses the necessity of keeping one's mind as clear of stain and irregular affection as one's actions are free of sin. "For," he asks, "of what avail is it to be a virgin in body, if one is not also a virgin in spirit?"[15]

Chapter XII

The Spirit of Sacrifice

WHEN speaking of the dispositions which should animate the celebrant of Holy Mass, St. Gregory wrote that "while we are engaged in this mystery we must immolate ourselves to God in contrition of heart, because when we celebrate the mysteries of our Lord's passion we must imitate what we do. For He will in all truth be for us a victim before God, if we make ourselves victims before Him."[1] St. Cyprian had written before him that the duty of priests, who daily offer sacrifice to God, is to prepare holocausts and victims for the Father.[2] The fundamental Christian principle of doing before preaching demands that the first of these victims and holocausts to the Father should be the priest himself. For this reason St. Gregory declares that the only man who can safely be charged with the spiritual welfare of others is one "who has died to all the passions of the flesh and now lives as a spiritual man."[3]

It is inescapable logic that if renunciation and sacrifice are the basic law of the Christian life, they must in a very special manner characterize the life of the spiritual leaders of the Church. Since man is constituted so largely by what is material and sensible, it is only through a process of separation and sacrifice that he can make room in his life for the spiritual and supernatural influences which should stand out in his activity. Going still farther we know that the essence of sin and virtue consists less in external actions than in the interior act of the will accepting evil or good. Similarly, the essence of Christian renunciation does not consist in actual physical separation from the things of the world, but rather in the interior spirit which lifts the heart and the affections to what is higher and more noble than the world. A man may possess a spirit of complete sacrifice in the midst of worldly things, and he may also be most unmortified in spirit even though he be the poorest of the poor. The aim of Christlike renunciation is to purify the mind and the soul for a clearer perception of the things of God, and this is why it is so all-embracing in its scope: "Everyone of you who does not renounce all that he possesses . . ."[4] Commenting on these words, St. Gregory observes that "it is not so difficult to re-nounce what we *have,* but it is very much indeed to give up what we *are.*"[5] Elsewhere in this homily, the same doctor indicates the spiritual and interior aim of all renunciation when he says:

"Unless a man denies himself, he can never ascend to God who is above him."[6]

Dwelling on the duties of the pastoral ministry, St. Gregory points out that there are two ways of taking up one's cross and following Jesus. Since the priest is made up of body and soul, his cross may be borne by either of these two elements of his nature and the saint finds in the Apostle of the Gentiles the perfect exemplification of this truth: "The cross can be carried in two ways, either when the body is mortified through abstinence, or when the soul is afflicted through compassion for one's neighbor. Let us consider how Paul took up his cross, he who said: 'I chastise my body and bring it into subjection lest perhaps after preaching to others I myself should be rejected.'[7] In these words on mortification of the body we have heard him speak of the cross of the flesh. Let us now hear him speak of the cross of the mind in compassion for his neighbor. He says: 'Who is weak and I am not weak? Who is made to stumble, and I am not inflamed?'[8]

"Perfect preacher that he was, he carried the cross in his body, that he might give an example of abstinence. And because he bore with all the hardships caused by the weakness of others, he also carried the cross in his heart."[9]

From these words of St. Gregory it is clear that corporal austerities do not constitute the essence of priestly sacrifice, any more than of Christian renunciation in general. There is no denying that they have their place in any ascetical program of life; the extent to which they are to be practised will depend on individual spiritual needs and personal generosity under the impulse of the inspirations of grace. As St. Jerome wrote in his letter to the priest, Paulinus, on the training of clerics: "A man should frequently keep watch with God, and often go to bed on an empty stomach."[10]

In another passage he warns against undue confi-

dence in a merely formalistic conception of mortification, and he calls attention to the spiritualizing influence which should pervade all acts of self-denial.
He even stigmatizes this undue confidence as super-
stition. He insists that the priest be natural and sensible in all kinds of mortification, while guarding
against self-seeking and vanity in a life of self-denial.
There are some practices of penance, he remarks with
a touch of sarcasm, which can be performed in private,
but because they do not attract any attention many
persons fail to regard them as mortifications. Unless
a man is natural and unpretentious even in his pen-
ances, he will be endeavoring to build up a reputation
for frugality while really remaining in the field of
self-indulgence.[11]

These observations of St. Jerome show that mortification of the body is not in itself a gauge or proof
of sanctity and nobility of soul. For this reason St.
John Chrysostom declares unhesitatingly that, over
and above bodily macerations, he exacts of the priest
a further proof of moral strength and generosity. Practices of mortification, he writes, serve no good purpose
for the priest unless he is likewise gifted with noble
and manly will power to withstand the hardships and
setbacks entailed by his service of others.

Consequently, the most fruitful mortifications of
priestly life are those encountered in the zealous discharge of the sacred ministry. There are unlimited
opportunities for sacrifice in the faithful and whole-
hearted performance of what the Fathers set down as
the main duties of priestly life: offering sacrifice, ad-

ministering the sacraments, preaching, teaching, rebuking and admonishing the wayward, praying, and being in constant attendance on the needs of the faithful. No small amount of sacrifice is exacted by the generous practice of those virtues which the Fathers list as the most becoming adornments of the priestly soul: the spirit of faith, charity, chastity, humility, meekness, zeal, and personal dignity. Speaking of the self-denial implied by fidelity to duty and the practice of priestly virtues, St. John Chrysostom says pointedly:

"To give up dainty food, choice drinks, or a soft bed is, as we know, easy for many men, especially for those of rougher temperament or who have been trained in this style of living from their early years. This is also true of those whom robust health or hard work has made familiar with this kind of life.

"But when it is a question of insults, injustice, sharp words, intentional or indeliberate sarcasm from inferiors, the groundless complaints and reproaches which are addressed to us by rulers or their subjects, few men there are who know how to put up with these crosses. In fact you will hardly find one or two in a thousand. You will often encounter men who are generous in the practice of corporal austerities, but who lose their heads and become worse than wild beasts when they have to face these other crosses. It is such men as these who must, above all, be kept from the sanctuary.

"Even though a bishop is not worn out with fasting or does not go barefoot, certainly this will occasion no harm to the faithful in general. But his bursts of temper will work incalculable harm on him and on his people. God has not threatened any punishment for those who do not practise bodily austerities, but the fires of hell will be the lot of those who allow themselves to be carried off by their pride."[12]

St. Francis de Sales once said that restraining an indignant retort, curbing the sharp word, showing unalterable patience and a spirit of constant generosity are all small virtues, but, he adds, they are signs of great virtue. Such virtues are unfailing evidence of a spirit of sacrifice, and the priest who practises them generously can be sure that he is fulfilling his duty of dying to himself and living a spiritual life. His reward will be his greater likeness to his Divine Model, for, as St. Jerome wrote to his spiritual daughter, Eustochium: "It is a difficult task, but one with a great reward, when we must be like the martyrs, like the Apostles, and like Christ."[13]

Chapter XIII

The Priest's Own Soul

ON THE priest, no less than on the ordinary faithful, there rests the fundamental obligation of the Christian life — that of saving his soul. Our Lord did not exclude His Apostles from the warning question: "What doth it profit a man if he gain the whole world and suffer the loss of his soul?" The priest is accountable to God for even a fuller measure of salvation by the very fact that his sacerdotal vocation has constituted him an official guide of the Church for the faithful.

Hence he must exemplify for his flock much more than the absolute minimum which he requires of them. Otherwise he runs the risk of seeing his teaching woefully neglected. Yet there are greater obstacles for him than for the ordinary faithful. His ministry brings him into constant contact with sin, and, as St. Augustine wrote, if he is not cautious he may easily fall victim to its contagion:

"I have known almost innumerable excellent and holy bishops, priests, deacons, and other ministers of the divine Sacraments. It seemed to me that their life was all the more admirable and worthy of praise, because of the greater difficulty of preserving goodness and holiness intact in the midst of all sorts of men and surrounded by the distractions of human life.

"These ministers are not in charge of men who are well but rather of those who are sick. Hence they must come in contact with the vices of people if they are to cure them, and they must first of all face the pestilence of sin before they can hope to quell it. In such surroundings it is most difficult to lead a well-ordered life and to keep one's soul calm and tranquil."[1]

Unfortunately, however, this foremost duty of every priest can too easily be forgotten. St. Paul manifested his own forebodings on this score when he expressed fear lest after preaching to others, he himself should be rejected. This explains St. Bernard's solemn exhortation to Pope Eugenius that in the business of salvation no one should be nearer to him than the only son of his mother. St. Gregory had already stressed this point in his homilies to the clergy, particularly in his *Regulae Pastoralis Liber*. After dwelling on the priest's duty of concern for the salvation of his people, the zealous Pope vividly turns his attention to the priest himself: "How can we reform the lives of others if we neglect our own? With our interests centered on worldly cares, we gradually become interiorly insensible, according as we seem to be more zealous in exterior occupations. Constant association with the things of earth deadens the soul to the desire of heavenly things, and because the soul is hardened by its activity, it cannot be softened to what pertains to the love of God."[2]

The same Doctor takes up this identical theme in even more graphic terms in his *Regulae Pastoralis Liber:* "When the soul is dragged abroad through needless activity, it is despoiled of the solid basis of interior fear. Busy with the organization of exterior things, it knows everything but itself, and is adept at thinking of many interests while it neglects itself. For when the soul becomes needlessly involved in external interests, it becomes, as it were, all intent on the road it is traveling and forgets its destination. Thus while it neglects self-examination, it does not even heed the losses it sustains and is unaware of how seriously it may be offending God."[3]

Continuing his realistic descriptions, St. Gregory has recourse to another expressive comparison: "The pastor must be always pure-minded, in order that no uncleanness may defile him who has assumed the office of cleansing others from the stains of defilement. For it behooves that hand to be clean which undertakes to wash away dirt. Let the pastor beware lest he make matters worse by trying to cleanse away dirt with muddy hands."[4]

Thus it is that so much of the efficacy of a priest's ministry depends on the holiness of his own life. By the same token, the sterility of priestly activity can frequently be explained by a lack of personal holiness in him who is devoting his time and talents to the sanctification of others. Drawing a parallel between the Old Law and the New, the *Regulae Pastoralis Liber* enumerates the crimes which excluded the Jewish priests from the sanctuary, and then makes the application to the priesthood of the New Dispensation: "Whoever is the slave of any one of these vices is excluded from offering loaves to the Lord, because no one is in a position to take away the sins of others if he is still being laid waste by his own."[5]

This great truth had inspired another figure in a preceding chapter: "If the priest's passions are still evident in his actions, how can he dare to hasten to treat another, when he still carries an open wound on his own face?"[6]

Long before St. Gregory, St. Ambrose had reminded his clergy that their sacred duty of self-interest must take precedence over all their other priestly activities:

"It is a beautiful thing for you to devote the grace which you have received and the benefit of your ministrations to the welfare of human society. But the first of all beautiful things is for you to consecrate to God your own mind, which is the most precious and most outstanding of all your possessions. For you can direct your activity toward the welfare and assistance of men, only after you have paid your own debt to your Creator."[7]

Meditation on the gospel phrase: "Physician, cure thyself!"[8] afforded the Fathers many points of comparison for their exhortations to priestly holiness as the foundation of all fruitful apostolic zeal. One of the most striking of these developments of the gospel theme comes from the pen of St. Ambrose:

"At the same time we are shown the portrait of the minister of Christ. He must, first of all, be free of the attractions of various pleasures and avoid internal sickness of both body and soul in order to minister the Body and Blood of Christ. No one who is sick with his own sins and not spiritually well can administer the medicine of everlasting health.

"Take heed what you do, O priest of God, and touch not the Body of Christ with a feverish hand. First cure yourself in order that you may minister to others. For if Christ orders those who were healed of leprosy to present themselves clean to the priest, with how much greater reason does it behoove the priest himself to be clean."[9]

Very beautifully St. Augustine bases the priest's obligation of living a holy life on the fact that many of his flock are imitating Christ, the Great Shepherd, and that, after all, under Christ the Shepherd and in His one great flock, even the human shepherds of the Church are as sheep.[10]

In the letter of St. Ignatius of Antioch to the Trallians we find how early the spirit of "in the world, but not of the world" had motivated the Church's bishops in their exhortations to their clergy. He writes: "It behooves the deacons, who are the ministers of the mysteries of Christ, to find favor with God in all things and in all ways. For they are not merely ministers of food and drink, but ministers of the Church of God. It behooves them, then, to flee from sin as from fire."[11]

The obligation of acquiring genuine holiness may easily be overlooked because of the great respect with which the priesthood is everywhere surrounded by the faithful. The whole attitude of the laity toward the priest is that of the Jews toward Abraham: "Thou art the prince of God among us!"[12] The nobility of his position can blind the priest into thinking, particularly if he is successful and popular, that he has already reached his goal in the eyes of God because the holiness of his position puts him on a pedestal of respect and reverence before the faithful. This was the warning of St. Jerome to Pammachius, lest he be unduly elated by knowing that he was being singled out for the priesthood: "I hear that the choice of the whole city has fallen upon you. I hear that the bishop and the people are in perfect agreement. Do not forget, however, that *it is easier to become a priest than to deserve to become one.*"[13]

So perfectly is personal holiness the foundation of the genuinely priestly life that whoever forgets this principal purpose of his existence has, in the solemn words of St. Bernard, lost sight of the chief reason which brought him to the sanctuary, because no unholy priest can find favor with God:

"But you, O priest of the Most High, whom are you endeavoring to please: the world, or God? If you are trying to please the world, why are you a priest? If you are trying to please God, why is it that your people follow your bad example? For if you are striving to find favor with the world, of what avail is your priesthood? You can not serve two masters. . . . In trying to please the world, you are displeasing to God: and if you do not please God, you can not placate Him (*Si non places, non placas*). Why, then, I ask, are you a priest?"[14]

The priest's fundamental duty of self-interest becomes all the more evident if we consider the multiplicity and the greatness of the dangers which beset him. Because his is a spiritual ministry, he must expect to face spiritual enemies. Unfortunately, we cannot exclude the possibility that the enemy may win out and triumph in the eternal loss of a priestly soul. Still it should not be forgotten that a realization of threatening danger is the most potent means of self-protection. Hence St. John Chrysostom draws the following picture of the dangers which beset the priest in the exercise of his ministry:

"Do you want to know who are the enemies against whom the priest must hurl his courage? Paul will tell you: 'Our wrestling is not against flesh and blood, but against the Principalities and the Powers, against the world-rulers of this darkness, against the spiritual forces of wickedness on high.'[15] Do you see this frightening horde of enemies drawn up in fearful battle-ranks? They are not armed with steel. No; their nature takes the place of all armor.

"Do you want to see other no less fierce legions who throw themselves against this flock? You will see them by the light of this same Torch.[16] He who told us of the first kind of enemies now describes the second: 'The works of the flesh are manifest, which are immorality, uncleanness, licentiousness, idolatry, witchcrafts, enmities, contentions, jealousies, anger, and disorders.'[17] It would be easy to carry out this list still farther. The Apostle did not say everything on this point, but leaves it for us to complete his thought.

"When there is question of an ordinary flock, those who want to destroy it do not bother to attack the shepherd if he runs away; they are satisfied with tearing it to pieces at their ease. But it is not the same in our case. Even when enemies have ravaged the entire flock, they do not leave the shepherd unharmed. On the contrary, they become all the more fierce and determined, and will give no quarter until they have either vanquished him or been routed by him."[18]

Insistence on the priest's duties of self-interest amid the grave perils of his ministry was not intended by the Fathers as spiritual defeatism. Rather it was an exhortation to untiring watchfulness and valor. When St. John Chrysostom summed up the priest's solemn duty of protecting himself against the enemy by writing that his only alternative is either to vanquish the devil or be routed by him, this was only his way of expressing the grim reality which a defense plant has embodied in a poster to arouse its employees to capacity production: "Remember! There is no second place in war!"

Conclusion

AT THE end of the *Regulae Pastoralis Liber* St.
Gregory the Great addresses his readers in words
which we may well repeat in concluding this study of
the Fathers' ideal of the priesthood:

"And now, my good friend, spurred on by the need
of self-reproach, in my efforts to point out for you
what the pastor should be, I have painted for you a
beautiful portrait, I who am only a mediocre artist.
I have been directing others to the shore of perfection,
while I myself was still tossed about on the waves of
sin. But, I beg of you, amidst the wreckage of this life,
keep me afloat with the plank of your prayers, in order
that, though my own weight carries me down, the
hand of your merits may hold me up."[1]

May all of God's priests reflect these noble ideals
in their own lives. May they thus fulfill the ardent
wish of the bishop who prayed at their ordination
that he would never have occasion to regret their pro-
motion to the priestly office. May they strive to be such
that, in the words of St. Jerome, "the bishop may rejoice in his judgment when he sees that he has chosen
such souls for Christ."[2]

Lastly we may echo St. Gregory's conclusion to his
inspiring homily on the priesthood:

"But we can obtain for you all these graces more surely by prayer than by exhortation:

"Let us pray

"O God, who hast willed that we should be called shepherds among Thy people; grant, we beseech Thee, that what we are called by the mouths of men, we may merit to be in Thine eyes. Through Christ our Lord. A M E N."[2]

Footnotes

AUTHOR'S PREFACE

[1] Hebr. 5:1.
[2] Ibid.
[3] Hebr. 5:3.

CHAPTER I

[1] Verse 26.
[2] St. Ignatius of Antioch, ad Polycarpum, no. 1; Funk, Patres Apostolici, I, 289.
[3] On the Priesthood, Bk. 6, no. 4; 2, 98 C. The system often used in Migne of indicating the position of a text in a column by the use of letters A, B, C, D, has been retained as useful even for those works or volumes in which these indications are not explicitly given.
[4] On the Priesthood, Bk. 3, no. 16; 2, 54 C.
[5] Regulae Pastoralis Liber, pars 1, cap. 10; 77, 23 A.
[6] B. Alcuin, Epistula 72 ad Simeonem Presbyterum; 100, 245 A.
[7] De Consideratione, lib. 4, cap. 6, no. 17; 182, 785 A.
[8] De Consideratione, lib. 4, cap. 7, no. 13; 182, 788 A.
[9] In Epistulam ad Ephesios, Lectio III, p. 8.

CHAPTER II

[1] Commentaria in omnes S. Pauli Apostoli Epistolas, ed. Marietti, Turin, 1929; II, 49.
[2] Ecclesiastical Review, Vol. 95, pp. 460–470, 593–600; Vol. 96, p. 65, pp. 178–182, 414–418, 531–535; Vol. 98, pp. 356–359, 466–468.
[3] Cf. e.g., Leo, Sermo 63, de Passione Domini XII, cap. 7; 54, 357

B; also St. Augustine, In Ioannem, tr. 21, no. 8; 35, 1568 B.
[4] Homily I on the Epistle to the Hebrews, no. 1; 20, 100 D.
[5] Gal. 5:16.
[6] Commentary on the Epistle to the Galatians, ch. 1, no. 9; 18, 83 B.
[7] Homily 13 on the Epistle to the Hebrews, no. 3; 20, 250 D.
[8] Homily 32 on St. Matthew, no. 3; 12, 122 B.
[9] Homily 14 on the Acts, no. 3; 14, 608 A.
[10] Homily 29 on the Epistle to the Romans, no. 2; 16, 270 B.
[11] Sermo 5, In Natali Ipsius V, cap. 4; 54, 154 C.
[12] In Ioannem, tract. 15, no. 3; 35, 1511 C.
[13] Epistle 14, no. 8; 22, 352 A.
[14] Homily 2 on the Second Epistle to Timothy, no. 2; 19, 548 B.
[15] On the Priesthood, Bk. 3, no. 6; 2, 36.
[16] 1:12.
[17] Homily 50 on St. Matthew, no. 3; 12, 351 A.
[18] On the Priesthood, Bk. 4, no. 2; 2, 72 D.
[19] Ephesians 5:26, 27.

CHAPTER III

[1] Homily 20 on the Epistle to the Romans, no. 2; 16, 165 B.
[2] Homily 20 on the Epistle to the Romans, no. 2; 16, 165 B.
[3] Epistula 63, no. 17; 4, 398 C.
[4] Epistula 6, cap. 3, no. 5; 13, 1166 B.
[5] Rom. 6:9.
[6] Dialogorum Libri, lib. 4, cap. 58; 77, 425 C.

[7] *De Civitate Dei*, lib. 10, cap. 20; 41, 298 B.

[8] *John* 8:12.

[9] *Epistula 63*, no. 14; 4, 397 B.

[10] *Epistula Synodica ad S. Cornelium PP.*, no. 3; 3, 884 A.

[11] *Dialogorum Libri*, lib. 4, cap. 56; 77, 421 C.

[12] *Dialogorum Libri*, lib. 4, cap. 59; 77, 428 A.

[13] Plutarch, *Vitae*, ed. Didot, Paris, 1872; Aemilius Paulus, no. 3; I, 306.

[14] *Sermo 79*, de Jejunio Pentecostes XII, cap. 1; 54, 418 B.

[15] *Homily on the Cemetery and the Cross*, no. 3; 4, 9 A.

[16] Msgr. Gay, *De la Vie et des Vertus Chrétiennes*, I, p. 171.

[17] *Epistula 60*, ad Heliodorum, no. 12; 22, 596 D.

[18] *Sermo 280*, no. 5: De Dominica et aliis diebus festis pie celebrandis; 39, 2275 D.

[19] *Divinae Institutiones*, lib. 6, cap. 25; 6, 730 B.

CHAPTER IV

[1] *John* 1:18.

[2] *Commentary on the Epistle to the Galatians*, I, no. 9; 18, 83 B.

[3] *Job* 7:1.

[4] *De Moribus et Officio Episcoporum*, cap. 1, No. 1; 182, 809 C.

[5] *Homily 3 on the Acts*, no. 4; 14, 471 B.

[6] *Hebr.* 5:1.

[7] *Hebr.* 13:17. *Homily 86 on St. John*, no. 4; 14, 404 B.

[8] *Hebr.* 13:17.

[9] *Matt.* 18:6.

[10] *Cor.* 8:12.

[11] *Ezech.* 33:3.

[12] *On the Priesthood*, Bk. 6, no. 1; 2, 94 C.

[13] *In Ps. 36*, Sermo 2, no. 1; 36, 363 C.

[14] Canon 1350, § 1.

[15] *On the Priesthood*, Bk. 2, 4; 2, 23 B.

[16] *On the Priesthood*, Bk. 4, no. 4; 2, 74 C.

[17] *Homily 10 on the First Epistle to the Thessalonians*, no. 1; 19, 289 C.

[18] *Homily 29 on the Epistle to the Romans*, no. 1; 16, 269 B.

CHAPTER V

[1] *Homily 17*, no. 17; 76, 1148 A.

[2] *Regulae Pastoralis Liber*, pars 2, cap. 3; 77, 29 C.

[3] *Regulae Pastoralis Liber*, pars 2, cap. 8; 77, 42 B.

[4] *In Ioannem*, tract. 36, no. 6; 35, 1666 C.

[5] *Regulae Pastoralis Liber*, pars 1, cap. 5; 77, 19 C.

[6] Cf. *3 Kings* 7:23 ff.

[7] *Regulae Pastoralis Liber*, pars 2, cap. 5; 77, 34 A.

[8] *Luke* 6:12.

[9] *Regulae Pastoralis Liber*, pars 2, cap. 5; 77, 33 B.

[10] *Regulae Pastoralis Liber*, pars 2, cap. 5; 77, 33 B.

[11] *1 Cor.* 9:16.

[12] *John* 1:18.

[13] *Luke* 4:43.

[14] *De Officiis Ministrorum*, lib. 3, cap. 9, no. 59; 16, 171 B.

[15] *In Psalm 44*, n. 20; 36, 507 B.

[16] *Homily 59 on St. Matthew*, no. 5; 12, 481 D.

[17] *Regulae Pastoralis Liber*, pars 1, cap. 4; 77, 17 C.

[18] *Regulae Pastoralis Liber*, pars 2, cap. 7; 77, 39 A.

[19] *Regulae Pastoralis Liber*, pars 2, cap. 8; 77, 42 C.

[20] *De Consideratione*, lib. 1, cap. 5, no. 6; 182, 734 A.

[21] *De Consideratione*, lib. 1, cap. 3, no. 4; 182, 732 A.

[22] *De Consideratione*, lib. 1, cap. 2, no. 3; 182, 730 B.

[23] *De Consideratione*, lib. 1, cap. 4; no. 5; 182, 733 B.

[24] *De Consideratione*, lib. 1, cap. 2, no. 2; 182, 730 A.

[25] *De Consideratione*, lib. 1, cap. 2, no. 3; 182, 731 A.

CHAPTER VI

[1] *Liber de Virginitate*, cap. 8; 16, 292 C.

[2] *Regulae Pastoralis Liber*, pars 2, cap. 1; 77, 25 D.

[3] *Tractatus de Moribus et Officio Episcoporum*, cap. 2, no. 5; 182, 815 A.

[4] *On the Priesthood*, Bk. 3, no. 14; 2, 47 A.

[5] *De Consideratione*, lib. 4, cap. 2, no. 3; 182, 773 D.

[6] *Homily 17*, no. 18; 76, 1149 B.

[7] *Homily 12*, no. 1; 76, 1119 A.

[8] *Collatio XI*, De Perfectione, cap. 4; 49, 851 B.

[9] *Regulae Pastoralis Liber*, pars 2, cap. 3; 77, 28 B.

[10] *De Virginibus*, lib. 3, cap. 1, no. 1; 16, 231 B.

[11] *In Joannem*, tractatus 46, no. 6; 35, 1730 C.

[12] *Epistula 52*, ad Nepotianum, no. 7; 22, 533 C.

[13] *De Consideratione*, lib. 2, cap. 7, no. 15; 182, 750 C.

[14] *Regulae Pastoralis Liber*, pars 3, cap. 4; 77, 54 B.

[15] *Regulae Pastoralis Liber*, pars 3, cap. 4; 77, 55 A.

[16] *Regulae Pastoralis Liber*, pars 3, cap. 4; 77, 54 D.

[17] *De Sermone Domini in Monte*, lib. 2, cap. 1, no. 3; 34, 1271 A.

[18] 24, 18–19.

[19] *Regulae Pastoralis Liber*, pars 1, cap. 2; 77, 15 D.

[20] *Regulae Pastoralis Liber*, pars 1, cap. 2; 77, 16 A.

[21] *De Coenobiorum Institutis*, lib. 4, cap. 6; 49, 159 B.

[22] *De Officiis Ministrorum*, lib. 1, cap. 50, no. 246; 16, 103 B.

[23] *De Officiis Ministrorum*, lib. 1, cap. 18, no. 72; 16, 49.

[24] *De Officiis Ministrorum*, lib. 2, cap. 7, no. 29; 16, 118 B.

[25] *Epistula 14*, ad Heliodorum, no. 9; 22, 353 B.

[26] *Homily 8*, no. 2; 76, 1105 A.

[27] *De Consideratione*, lib. 4, cap. 3, no. 6; 182, 776 A.

[28] *Epistula 69*, ad Oceanum, no. 9; 22, 664 B.

CHAPTER VII

[1] *De Consideratione*, lib. 2, cap. 6, no. 13; 182, 750 A.

[2] *Tractatus de Moribus et Officio Episcoporum*, cap. 5, no. 20; 182, 822 D.

[3] *Regulae Pastoralis Liber*, pars 2, cap. 6; 77, 35 A.

[4] *Regulae Pastoralis Liber*, pars 1, cap. 9; 77, 22 A.

[5] *Regulae Pastoralis Liber*, pars 1, cap. 8; 77, 21 C.

[6] *Regulae Pastoralis Liber*, pars 1, cap. 7; 77, 20 D.

[7] *Regulae Pastoralis Liber*, pars 1, cap. 3; 77, 16 C.

[8] *Regulae Pastoralis Liber*, pars 1, cap. 4; 77, 18 B.

[9] *Regulae Pastoralis Liber*, pars 1, cap. 6; 77, 19 D.

[10] *Regulae Pastoralis Liber*, pars 1, cap. 7; 77, 20 D.

[11] *Homily Against Cursing*, no. 4; 2, 523 B.

[12] *Regulae Pastoralis Liber*, pars 4; 77, 127 A.

[13] *Regulae Pastoralis Liber*, pars 2, cap. 10; 77, 46 B.

[14] *Regulae Pastoralis Liber*, pars 2, cap. 8; 77, 43 B.

[15] *Homily on Peter the Apostle and Isaias the Prophet*, no. 1; IV, 516 D.

[16] *Regulae Pastoralis Liber*, pars 2, cap. 6; 77, 36 D.

[17] *Homily 13 on the First Epistle to Timothy*, no. 1; 19, 473 C.

[18] *Homily 4 on the Epistle to the Colossians*, no. 4; 19, 66 D.

[19] *Homily 13 on the First Epistle to Timothy*, no. 1; 19, 472 D.

[20] *Homily 17*, no. 12; 76, 1144 D.

[21] *Moralium Libri*, lib. 20, cap. 5, no. 14; 76, 143 C.

[22] *Regulae Pastoralis Liber*, pars 2, cap. 6; 77, 37 A.

[23] *Regulae Pastoralis Liber*, pars 2, cap. 6; 77, 35 C.

[24] ". . . et ne sub magnitudine gratiae succumbat infirmus, dabit virtutem qui contulit dignitatem." With these words from St. Leo, both Leo XIII and Pius X exhort whoever is elected to the Chair of Peter not to refuse the burden for fear of the weight of responsibility. (Constitution, *Vacante Sede Apostolica*, cap. VI, n. 86.)

[25] *Sermo 2, In Natali Ipsius II;* cap. 1; 54, 142 C.
[26] *Sermo 3, In Natali Ipsius III,* cap. 1; 54, 144 B.
[27] . . . nec praeesse se hominibus gaudeant, sed prodesse. *Homily 17,* no. 4; 76, 1140 B.
[28] *Regulae Pastoralis Liber,* pars 2, cap. 6; 77, 34 C.

CHAPTER VIII
[1] *On the Priesthood,* Bk. IV, no. 2; 2, 73 A.
[2] *Homily 15 on the First Epistle to Timothy,* no. 2; 19, 503 A.
[3] *Regulae Pastoralis Liber,* pars 1, no. 1; 77, 14 A.
[4] *Regulae Pastoralis Liber,* pars 1, cap. 1; 77, 15 B.
[5] *Regulae Pastoralis Liber,* pars 3, cap. 11; 77, 48 C.
[6] *In Aggaeum* (cap. 2, v. 11) ; 25, 1406 B.
[7] Mal. 1:7.
[8] *Epistula 69,* ad Fabiolam, no. 1; 22, 609 A.
[9] *Epistula 59,* ad Clerum et Plebem Constantinopolitanae Urbis, cap. 1; 54, 867 B.
[10] *On the Priesthood,* Bk. 4, no. 5; 2, 77 A.
[11] *Epistula 4,* ad Episcopos Provinciae Viennensis, cap. 2; 50, 431 B.
[12] *Epistula 68,* ad Oceanum, no. 9; 22, 663 B.
[13] *Epistula 52,* ad Nepotianum, no. 8; 22, 534 C.
[14] *In Aggaeum* (cap. 2, v. 11); 25, 1407 B.
[15] *Regulae Pastoralis Liber,* pars 2, cap. 11; 77, 49 A.
[16] *Epistula 60,* ad Heliodorum, no. 11; 22, 595 D.

CHAPTER IX
[1] *De Consideratione,* lib. 2, cap. 13, no. 22; 182, 756 B.
[2] *De Consideratione,* lib. 3, cap. 5, no. 19; 182, 771 A.
[3] *Epistula 22,* ad Eustochium, no. 28; 22, 414 A.
[4] *Epistula 52,* ad Nepotianum, no. 15; 22, 539 A.

[5] *Epistula 52,* ad Nepotianum, no. 11; 22, 536 C.
[6] *On the Priesthood,* Bk. 6, no. 5; 2, 99 D.
[7] *Homily 85 on St. Matthew,* no. 4; 13, 177 C.
[8] *On the Priesthood,* Bk. 3, no. 18; 2, 61 D.
[9] 21:2.
[10] *Homily 31,* no. 8; 76, 1231 D.
[11] *De Officiis Ministrorum,* lib. I, cap. 14, no. 66; 16, 127 C.
[12] *Epistula 52,* ad Nepotianum, no. 5; 22, 531 passim.
[13] *Tractatus de Moribus et Officio Episcoporum,* cap. 3, no. 11; 182, 817 C.

CHAPTER X
[1] *In Lucae Evangelium Expositio,* cap. 12; 92, 494 D.
[2] 1 Tim. 6:10.
[3] 1 Cor. 16:1-4; 2 Cor. 9:1-5.
[4] 1 Cor. 9:1-14; 2 Cor. 11:1-6.
[5] 1 Tim. 6:6.
[6] 1 Tim. 6:8-9.
[7] *Homily 15 on the Epistle to the Corinthians,* no. 5; 16, 517 D.
[8] 2 Thess. 3:10.
[9] *Homily 21 on the Epistle to the Corinthians,* no. 3; 16, 598 A.
[10] *Homily 22 on the Epistles to the Corinthians,* no. 1; 16, 611 D.
[11] *Homily 15 on the First Epistle to Timothy,* no. 2; 19, 501 D.
[12] Ecclus. 3:13.
[13] Matt. 10:9.
[14] 1 Tim. 6:8.
[15] *Homily 9 on the Epistle to the Philippians,* no. 4; 18, 566 D.
[16] *On the Priesthood,* Bk. 3, no. 16; 2, 57 D.
[17] *Epistula 52,* ad Nepotianum, no. 6; 22, 533 A.
[18] *Epistula 52,* ad Nepotianum, no. 6; 22, 533 A.
[19] *De Officiis Ministrorum,* lib. 1, cap. 16; 16, 130 C.
[20] *Epistula 52,* ad Nepotianum, no. 9; 22, 535 B.
[21] *De Officiis Ministrorum,* lib. 1, cap. 36, no. 184; 16, 83 B.
[22] *Sermo 37,* ad Fratres in Eremo, 40, 1301 D.

CHAPTER XI

[1] *Tractatus de Moribus et Officio Episcoporum,* cap. 3, no. 8; 182, 816 C.

[2] *Tractatus de Moribus et Officio Episcoporum,* cap. 3, no. 8; 182, 817 A.

[3] Cf. Matt. 22:30.

[4] *Sermo 132,* cap. 3; 38, 736 B.

[5] *De Officiis Ministrorum,* lib. 1, cap. 50, no. 248; 16, 105 A.

[6] *Sermo 132,* cap. 3; 38, 736 B.

[7] *Epistula 14,* ad Anastasium, cap. 3; 54, 672 B.

[8] *Epistula 52,* ad Nepotianum, no. 5; 22, 531 D.

[9] *On the Priesthood,* Bk. 6, no. 8; 2, 104 D.

[10] Gal. 2:20.

[11] *On the Priesthood,* Bk. 6, no. 2; 2, 95 C.

[12] No. 1; 20, 14 D.

[13] *De Cultu Feminarum,* lib. 2, cap. 13; 1, 1447 A.

[14] *Ad Uxorem,* lib. 1, cap. 7; 1, 1397 A.

[15] *Regula Coenobialis,* c. 6; 80, 211 D.

CHAPTER XII

[1] *Dialogorum Libri,* lib. 4, cap. 59; 77, 428 A.

[2] *Epistula synodica ad S. Cornelium PP.,* no. 3; 3, 884 A.

[3] *Regulae Pastoralis Liber,* pars 1, cap. 10; 77, 23 A.

[4] Luke 14:33.

[5] *Homily 32,* no. 1; 76, 1233 A.

[6] *Homily 32,* no. 2; 76, 1234 A.

[7] 1 Cor. 9:27.

[8] 2 Cor. 11:29.

[9] *Homily 32,* no. 3; 76, 1234 B.

[10] Quoted by Amalarius of Metz in his *Regula Canonicorum,* cap. 95; 105, 887 B.

[11] *Epistula 52,* no. 12; 22, 538 B.

[12] *On the Priesthood,* Bk. 3, no. 13; 2, 45 B.

[13] *Epistula 22,* ad Eustochium, no. 38; 22, 422 D.

CHAPTER XIII

[1] *De Moribus Ecclesiae Catholicae,* lib. 1, cap. 32, no. 69; 32, 1339 C.

[2] *Homily 17,* no. 14; 76, 1146 B.

[3] *Regulae Pastoralis Liber,* pars 1, no. 4; 77, 17 C.

[4] *Regulae Pastoralis Liber,* pars 2, no. 2; 77, 27 A.

[5] *Regulae Pastoralis Liber,* pars 1, no. 11; 77, 26 C.

[6] *Regulae Pastoralis Liber,* pars 1, no. 9; 77, 22 D.

[7] *De Officiis Ministrorum,* lib. 1, cap. 50, no. 252; 16, 107 A.

[8] Luke 4:23.

[9] *Liber de Viduis,* cap. 10, no. 65; 16, 267 A.

[10] *In Ioannem,* tract. 123, no. 5; 35, 1969 B.

[11] *Ad Trallianos,* Funk, *Patres Apostolici,* II; 1, 245.

[12] Gen. 23:6.

[13] *Epistula 49,* ad Pammachium, no. 4; 22, 512 A.

[14] *Tractatus de Moribus et Officio Episcoporum,* cap. 2, no. 5; 182, 814 A.

[15] Eph. 6:12.

[16] St. John Chrysostom uses the term "The Torch" to signify St. Paul.

[17] Gal. 5:19–21; 2 Cor. 12:20.

[18] *On the Priesthood,* Bk. 2, no. 2; 2, 20 A.

CONCLUSION

[1] *Regulae Pastoralis Liber,* pars 4, Conclusio; 77, 128 A.

[2] *Epistula 52,* ad Nepotianum, no. 7; 22, 534 B.

[3] *Homily 17,* no. 18; 76, 1149 C.

Index

167